Modern One-act Plays

Model Interpretations

Tom Stoppard · James Saunders
Harold Pinter

By Horst Buss, Bruno von Lutz
and Kunibert Schäfer

Ernst Klett Stuttgart

Acknowledgments

H. Pinter. *A Slight Ache* from *A Slight Ache and Other Plays* (1961) is reprinted by permission of Eyre Methuen Ltd., London.

J. Saunders. *A Slight Accident* from *Neighbours and Other Plays* (1964) is reprinted by permission of Andre Deutsch Ltd., London.

T. Stoppard, *A Separate Peace* from *Playbill Two,* ed. Alan Durband, 1969, is reprinted by permission of Fraser & Dunlop Scripts Ltd., London.

The texts to which these interpretations refer are also available in a student's edition: Modern One-act Plays (Klettbuch 5783).

A recorded version of the one-act plays interpreted here is available on cassette (Klettnummer 57837).

1. Auflage 1 4 3 2 1 | 1983 82 81 80

Alle Drucke dieser Auflage können im Unterricht nebeneinander benutzt werden. Die letzte Zahl bezeichnet das Jahr dieses Druckes.

Umschlaggestaltung: Hans Lämmle, Stuttgart.
Druck: Wilhelm Röck, Weinsberg. Printed in Germany.
ISBN 3-12-578330-5

Contents

Preface to the Students' Book

The theatre is one of the liveliest arts in contemporary Britain, and in recent years there has been a renaissance in the provincial theatre. Hand in hand with this new interest in drama, the one-act play has shown itself to be an adaptable and popular form.
The one-act plays in this collection are by three of today's leading British dramatists.

The phonetic transcription in the *Annotations* is from Jones-Gimson, *English Pronouncing Dictionary*, 14th edition. The following abbreviations are used in the *Annotations:*

A.E.	American English	*poet.*	poetic
cf.	confer, see	*sg.*	singular
coll.	colloquial	*sl.*	slang
etc.	and so on, *et cetera*	*s.o.*	someone
o.s.	oneself	*s.th.*	something
pl.	plural		

Numbers in bold-face type in the margin refer to the corresponding pages in the text, those in light-face type to the lines of the respective page.
Example: **4** 27 = page 4, line 27.

Introduction

True, one can read a playscript like a novel or a short story, mainly for the sake of the story, and still derive a great deal of pleasure from it. But the reader of a play can also enjoy infinitely more than the mere development of a story; he can and should try to form vivid impressions of theatrical action, since there is more to a play than just the script. One should always remember that it was not intended for reading, or for reading alone. When reading a play, our eyes merely follow the lines on the page, but when we see a play, several sensations can be experienced at the same time: we hear words being spoken, see actors moving, their expressions changing, and perhaps hear special sound effects. Ronald Hayman once said about reading plays, "It's like reading a painter's description of his picture instead of looking at the canvas."[1] Therefore, while studying a play, the reader has to perform the double task of reading the text and at the same time transforming the information he gets from it into a mental image. If one does not witness an actual performance, this is a difficult task, and a good result can only be achieved if we constantly remind ourselves that the script of a play is always intended to be "a score for theatrical impacts."[2] Often it can be helpful to read the play aloud either just by oneself, or sharing the dialogue with others. It is therefore recommended that the students read some passages aloud in the classroom and that they listen to the recorded versions available on cassette. If this is done, the students will be better able to appreciate the humour in the plays and will get a more vivid impression of the dialogue as well as of the function and quality of silences and pauses.

The stage dimension has been given considerable space in the interpretations in this book. The other elements of drama regularly dealt with are plot, character and language. The following general remarks on procedure might prove useful to the teacher.[3]

In recent years, the importance of "gestaltendes Lesen" has been stressed. But at the same time we should recognise that the majority of pupils (at the age of 16 or more) are not too co-operative when it comes to

1 Ronald Hayman, *How to Read a Play*, London 1977, p.12
2 *Ibid*, p. 15
3 These notes should be considered supplementary to the many useful suggestions made in the various contributions in *Der Fremdsprachliche Unterricht* 49 (1979), "Hörspiel und Kurzdrama", which we highly recommend.

reading a text aloud (let alone assuming the role of a character) in front of the other members of a course. This obstacle might be overcome by the use of a tape recorder: groups of pupils could be assigned different passages of the play which they are to record at home and which are then to be played back in the classroom. This will enable the teacher to make his pupils (re-) create the atmosphere of a play (remember that Pinter's *A Slight Ache* was originally conceived as a radio play) and make them sensitive to the importance of careful play reading and, above all, to the importance of closely following stage directions such as "Silence", "Pause", and the different tones of voice in which some passages must be rendered. Another way to achieve the same aim would be to ask two or more groups of pupils to record the same passage: a comparison of different "versions" might provoke even an inattentive student into reacting, because the class will be asked to decide which of the recordings is the best. The pupils' recordings could also be compared with those available on cassette and differences in interpretation can be discussed.

The analyses suggested in the units are based on the assumption that, before talking about the text in the classroom, the students have already read it on their own. If this has not been the case, the teacher should present the opening scenes of the play under discussion from the cassette. Besides being a useful listening comprehension exercise, this method may have other advantages. The opening passages of *A Slight Ache* as recorded on the cassette, for example, will reveal the rather chilly family life of Edward and Flora much better than would a perfunctory reading in the classroom or at home. The pupils' books should remain closed during the first listening, and the teacher should provide a vocabulary list for the passages in question.

Many modern (one-act) plays have been classified as "absurd" – a misnomer, which is all too readily applied to any piece of literature that allows several different interpretations because of (or thanks to) either the author's deliberate disregard for convention, (such as the cause-and-effect structure of the category "plot") or his refusal to provide the reader/spectator with categorical statements about the "meaning" of his play. This state of affairs can have two opposite effects:

On the one hand, it may arouse the pupils' curiosity – there may be a variety of solutions, all of them valid, to one problem, so a conflict between different interpretations seems inevitable. The result of such conflicts occurring in class will hopefully be a discussion, in which all the members of a course should be given ample opportunity to state their opinions. In this way, the "absurd" nature of modern one-act plays can contribute to the motivation of the students. Needless to say, conflict situations, which urge interested pupils to argue about the best solution possible, and which may even get usually inattentive students to join in, are extremely welcome in the classroom.

On the other hand, the difficulty of solving the problem of how to interpret a play or passages from a play may discourage even the good students: the phenomenon that, in many modern plays, there is more than just one valid interpretation may frustrate them and cause them to lose interest in any spontaneous discussion about the play. In this situation, the teacher plays an important role: his function must be that of a mediator, who accepts, and encourages his pupils to accept, different interpretations as long as evidence for them is provided in the text. But this, too, might unfortunately mean interrupting students who jump to conclusions without textual support. We suggest that, at the beginning of a lesson/unit, the teacher should start with a brief "brainstorming" session, during which he encourages the pupils to state their opinion on what they think the text offers; note things on the blackboard without attempting to evaluate them (for some students, once criticized, might be deterred from defending their position and thus exclude themselves from any further discussion); and then, with the visual aid of the blackboard in front of the students, he should proceed to a close scrutiny of the text under discussion. In doing so, he should pay special attention to the suggestions of the students. He should work towards what can be almost unanimously agreed on, and should make a clear distinction between this "common core" and the questions that remain open. This "common core" is important in two respects: a) It can act as a fitting conclusion to a discussion that may have got out of hand due to wild speculation; b) It will satisfy those students who are always keen on taking home "something concrete", i.e. an interpretation they can reproduce in future oral or written tests.

The various "units" or interpretative steps in this book need not be slavishly followed. It is left to the discretion of the teacher whether he wants to deal with all of them or to leave out certain aspects, for example when teaching a "Grundkurs". The individual units are graded in such a way that they tend to develop the students' interpretative abilities. For this reason a *Glossary of Literary Terms* has been included in the pupils' book; at all stages of the discussion, the pupils should be encouraged to make ample use of it. The Glossary might be particularly useful if the discussion of a one-act play is considered a preparatory stage to the reading of full-length plays. The extensive vocabulary lists in the pupils' book will facilitate a thorough preparation of the text at home so that sufficient time will be available for discussion in the classroom.

Tom Stoppard

A Separate Peace

Scene 1 *(The office of the Beechwood Nursing Home. Behind the reception counter sits a uniformed nurse. It is 2.30 a.m. A car pulls up outside. John Brown enters. He is a biggish man in his late forties, with a well-lined face: calm, pleasant, implacable. He is wearing a nondescript suit and overcoat, and carrying two zipped grips. Looking around, he notes the neatness, the quiet, the flowers, the nice nurse, and is quietly pleased.)*

BROWN Very nice.

NURSE Good evening . . .

BROWN 'Evening. A lovely night. Morning.

NURSE Yes . . . Mr . . .?

BROWN I'm sorry to be so late.

NURSE *(shuffling papers)* Were you expected earlier?

BROWN No. I telephoned.

NURSE Yes?

BROWN Yes.

NURSE I mean . . .?

BROWN You have a room for Mr Brown.

NURSE *(realisation)* Oh! – Have you brought him?

BROWN I brought myself. Knocked up a taxi by the station.

NURSE *(puzzled)* But surely . . .?

BROWN I telephoned, from the station.

NURSE You said it was an emergency.

BROWN That's right. Do you know what time it is?

NURSE It's half past two.

BROWN That's right. An emergency.

NURSE *(aggrieved)* I woke the house doctor.

BROWN A kind thought. But it's all right. Do you want me to sign in?

NURSE What is the nature of your emergency, Mr Brown?

BROWN I need a place to stay.

NURSE Are you ill?

BROWN No.

NURSE But this is a private hospital . . .

(Brown smiles for the first time.)

BROWN The best kind. What is a hospital without privacy? It's the privacy I'm after – that and the clean linen. . . . *(A thought strikes him.)* I've got money.

NURSE . . . the Beechwood Nursing Home.

BROWN I require nursing. I need to be nursed for a bit. Yes. Where do I sign?

NURSE I'm sorry, but admissions have to be arranged in advance except in the case of a genuine emergency – I have no authority –

BROWN What do you want with authority? A nice girl like you. *(Moves)* Where have you put me?

NURSE *(moves with him)* And *you* have no authority –

BROWN *(halts)* That's true. That's one thing I've never had. *(He looks at her flatly.)* I've come a long way.

NURSE *(wary)* Would you wait just one moment?

BROWN *(relaxes)* Certainly. Have you got a sign-in chit? Must abide by the regulations. Should I pay in advance?

NURSE No, that's quite all right.

BROWN I've got it – I've got it all in here –

(He starts trying to open one of the zipped cases, it jams and he hurts his finger. He recoils sharply and puts his finger in his mouth. The doctor arrives, dishevelled from being roused.)

NURSE Doctor – this is Mr Brown.

DOCTOR Good evening. What seems to be the trouble?

BROWN Caught my finger.

DOCTOR May I see?

(Brown holds out his finger, the doctor studies it, looks up. Guardedly)

Have you come far?

BROWN Yes. I've been travelling all day.

(The doctor glances at the nurse.)

BROWN Not with my finger. I did that just now. Zip stuck.

DOCTOR Oh. And what – er –

NURSE Mr Brown says there's nothing wrong with him.

BROWN That's right – I –

NURSE He just wants a bed.

BROWN A room.

DOCTOR But this isn't a hotel.

BROWN Exactly.

DOCTOR Exactly what?

BROWN I don't follow you.

DOCTOR Perhaps I'm confused. You see, I was asleep.

BROWN It's all right. I understand. Well, if someone would show me to my room, I shan't disturb you any further.

DOCTOR *(with a glance at the nurse)* I don't believe we have any rooms free at the moment.

BROWN Oh yes, this young lady arranged it.

NURSE *(self-defence)* He telephoned from the station. He said it was an emergency.

BROWN I missed my connection.

DOCTOR But you've come to the wrong place.

BROWN No, this is the place all right. I don't want to be a nuisance.

DOCTOR Did you try the pubs in the town?

BROWN I'm not drunk.

DOCTOR They have rooms.

BROWN I've got a room. What's the matter?

DOCTOR *(pause)* Nothing – nothing's the matter. *(He nods at the nurse.)* All right.

NURSE Yes, doctor. *(Murmurs worriedly)* I'll have to make an entry . . .

DOCTOR Observation.

BROWN *(cheerfully)* I'm not much to look at.

NURSE Let me take those for you, Mr Brown. *(The cases)*

BROWN No, no, don't you. *(Picks up cases)* There's nothing the matter with me. . . .

(Brown follows the nurse inside. The doctor watches them go, picks up Brown's form, and reads it. Then he picks up the phone and starts to dial.)

Scene 2 *(Brown's private ward. A pleasant room with a hospital bed and the usual furniture. One wall is almost all window and is curtained. Brown and the nurse enter. Brown puts his cases on the bed. He likes the room.)*

BROWN That's nice. I'll like it here.

NURSE Will you be all right?

BROWN Oh yes, I'm all right now. Picture window.

NURSE The bathroom is across the corridor.

BROWN *(peering through curtains)* What's the view?

NURSE Well, it's the drive and the gardens.

BROWN Gardens. A front room. What could be nicer?

(Nurse starts to open case.)

NURSE Are your night things in here?

BROWN Yes, I'll be very happy here.

(Nurse opens the case, which is full of money – bank notes.)

NURSE Oh – I'm sorry –

(Brown is not put out at all.)

BROWN What time is breakfast?

NURSE Eight o'clock.

BROWN Lunch?

NURSE Twelve o'clock.

BROWN Tea?

NURSE Three o'clock.

BROWN Supper?

NURSE Half past six.

BROWN Cocoa?

NURSE Nine.

BROWN Matron's rounds twice a day?

NURSE Yes.

BROWN Temperatures?

NURSE *(turning back his bed)* Morning and evening.

BROWN Change of sheets?

NURSE Monday.

BROWN Like clockwork. Lovely.

(The doctor enters with Brown's form and Elastoplast.)

DOCTOR Excuse me.

BROWN I was just saying – everything's A1.

DOCTOR I remembered your finger.

BROWN I'd forgotten myself. It's nothing.

DOCTOR Well, we'll just put this on overnight.

(He administers Elastoplast.)

BROWN Must be wonderful to have the healing touch. I should get to bed now – you look tired.

DOCTOR Thank you. I expect Matron will be along to discuss your case with you tomorrow.

BROWN My finger?

DOCTOR ... Well, I expect she'd like to meet you.

BROWN Be pleased to meet her.

DOCTOR Yes ... A final point, Mr Brown. This form you filled in ... Where it says permanent address, you've put down Beechwood Nursing Home.

BROWN Yes. Well, you never know what the future brings, but for the while I like to think of it as home....

Scene 3 *(The hospital office. It is morning, and the doctor is at the desk, telephoning.)*

DOCTOR ... I have absolutely no idea ... The nurse said it looked like several hundred pounds. ... His savings, yes. Frankly, I wouldn't be too keen on that – I don't really want the police turning up at the bedside of any patient who doesn't arrive with a life history. ... I think we'd get more out of him than you would, given a little time, and we'd certainly keep you informed ... No, he's not being difficult at all. ... You don't need to worry about that – he doesn't seem very keen to run away. He seems quite happy....

Scene 4 *(Brown's private ward. Brown is in striped pyjamas, eating off a tray. A second nurse – Nurse Coates (Maggie) – is waiting for him to finish so that she can take his tray away. Maggie is pretty and warm.)*

BROWN The point is not breakfast in bed, but breakfast in bed without guilt. Rich men's wives can bring it off, but if you're not a rich man's wife then you've got to be ill. Lunch in bed is more difficult, even for the rich. It's not any more expensive, but the disapproval is harder to ignore. To stay in bed for tea is almost impossible in decent society, and not to get up at all would probably bring in the authorities. Even if you had the strength of character there's probably a point where it becomes certifiable. But in a hospital it's not only understood – it's expected. That's the beauty of it. I'm not saying it's a great discovery – it's obvious really: but I'd say I'd got something.

MAGGIE If you'd got something, there wouldn't be all this fuss.

BROWN Is there a fuss? *(Maggie doesn't answer.)* They should leave well alone. I'm paying my way. ... Are you pretty full all the time?

MAGGIE Not at the moment, not very.

BROWN You'd think a place as nice as this would be very popular.

MAGGIE Popular?

BROWN I thought I might have to wait for a place, you know. Of course, it's a bit out of the way, no passing trade, so to speak. I'm very fond of the English countryside myself.

MAGGIE Where do you live?

BROWN I've never lived. Only stayed.

MAGGIE You should settle down somewhere.

BROWN Yes, I've been promising myself this.

MAGGIE Have you got a family?

BROWN I expect so.

MAGGIE Where are they?

BROWN I lost touch.

MAGGIE You should find them.

BROWN *(smiles)* Their name's Brown.

(The matron enters: she is not too old, and quite equable.)

MATRON Good morning.

BROWN Good morning to you. You must be matron.

MATRON That's right.

BROWN I must congratulate you on your hospital, it's a lovely place you run here. Everyone is so nice.

MATRON Well, thank you, Mr Brown. I'm glad you feel at home.

(Maggie takes Brown's tray.)

BROWN I never felt it there. Very good breakfast. Just what the doctor ordered. I hope he got a bit of a lie-in.

(Maggie exits with the tray, closing the door.)

MATRON Now, what's your problem, Mr Brown?

BROWN I have no problems.

MATRON Your complaint.

BROWN I have no complaints either. Full marks.

MATRON Most people who come here have something the *matter* with them.

BROWN That must give you a lot of extra work.

MATRON But it's what we're here for. You see, you can't really stay unless there's something wrong with you.

BROWN I can pay.

MATRON That's not the point.

BROWN What is the point?

MATRON This is a hospital. What are you after?

BROWN *(sadly)* My approach is too straightforward. An ordinary malingerer or a genuine hypochondriac wouldn't have all this trouble. They'd be accepted on their own terms. All I get is a lot of personal questions. *(Hopefully)* Maybe I could *catch* something ... But what difference would it make to you?

MATRON We have to keep the beds free for people who need them.

BROWN I need this room.

MATRON I believe you, Mr Brown – but wouldn't another room like this one do? – somewhere else? You see, we deal with physical matters – of the body –

BROWN There's nothing wrong with my *mind.* You won't find my name on any list.

MATRON I know.

BROWN *(teasing)* How do you know? *(She doesn't answer.)* Go for the obvious, it's worth considering. I know what I like: a nice atmosphere – good food – clean rooms – a day and night service – no demands – cheerful staff – Well, it's *worth* thirty guineas a week. I won't be any trouble.

MATRON Have you thought of going to a nice country hotel?

BROWN Different kettle of fish altogether. I want to do nothing, and have nothing expected of me. That isn't possible out there. It worries them. They want to know what you're at – staying in your room all the time – they want to know what you're *doing.* But in a hospital it is understood that you're not doing anything, because everybody's in the same boat – it's the normal thing. Being a patient. That's what I'm cut out for, I think – I've got a vocation for it.

MATRON But there's nothing wrong with you!

BROWN That's why I'm *here.* If there was something wrong with me I could get into any old hospital – free. As it is, I'm quite happy to pay for *not* having anything wrong with me. If I catch something, perhaps I'll transfer. I don't know, though. I like it here. It depends on how my money lasts. I wouldn't like to go to a city hospital.

MATRON But what do you want to do here?

BROWN Nothing.

MATRON You'll find that very boring.

BROWN One must expect to be bored, in hospital.

MATRON Have you been in hospital quite a lot?

BROWN No. I've been saving up for it. . . .

(He smiles.)

Scene 5 *(The hospital office. The doctor is phoning at a desk.)*

DOCTOR No luck? . . . Oh. Well, I don't know. The only plan we've got is to bore him out of here, but he's disturbingly self-sufficient. . . . Mmm, we've had a psychiatrist over ... Well, he seemed amused ... Both of them, actually; they were both amused . . . No, I shouldn't do that, he won't tell you anything. And there's one of our nurses – she's getting on very well with him . . . something's bound to come out soon . . .

Scene 6 *(Brown's ward. Brown is in bed with a thermometer in his mouth. Maggie is taking his pulse. She removes the thermometer, scans it and shakes it.)*

MAGGIE I'm wasting my time here, you know.

BROWN *(disappointed)* Normal?

MAGGIE You'll have to do better than that if you're going to stay.

BROWN You're breaking my heart, Maggie.

MAGGIE *(almost lovingly)* Brownie, what are you going to do with yourself?

BROWN Maggie, Maggie . . . Why do you want me to do something?

MAGGIE They've all got theories about you, you know.

BROWN Theories?

MAGGIE Train-robber.

BROWN That's a good one.

MAGGIE A spy from the Ministry.

BROWN Ho ho.

MAGGIE Embezzler.

BROWN Naturally.

MAGGIE Eccentric millionaire.

BROWN Wish I was. I'd have my own hospital, just for myself. I'd have the whole thing – with wards all named after dignitaries you've never heard of – and nurses, doctors, specialists, West Indian charladies, trolleys, rubber floors, sterilised aluminium, flowers, stretchers parked by the lifts, clean towels and fire regulations. . . . All built round me and staffed to feed me and check me and tick me off on a rota system.

MAGGIE It's generally agreed you're on the run.

BROWN No, I've stopped.

MAGGIE Fixations have been mentioned.

BROWN But you know better.

MAGGIE I think you're just lazy.

BROWN I knew you were the clever one.

MAGGIE *(troubled, soft)* Tell me what's the matter, Brownie?

BROWN I would if there was.

MAGGIE What do you want to stay here for then?

BROWN I like you.

MAGGIE You didn't know I was here.

BROWN That's true. I came for the quiet and the routine. I came for the white calm, meals on trays and quiet efficiency, time passing and bringing nothing. That seemed enough. I never got it down to a person. But I like you – I like you very much.

MAGGIE Well, I like you too, Brownie. But there's more in life than that.

(Matron enters.)

MATRON Good morning.

BROWN Good morning, matron.

MATRON And how are we this morning?

BROWN We're very well. How are you?

MATRON *(slightly taken aback)* *I'm* all right, thank you. Well, are you enjoying life?

BROWN Yes thank you, matron.

MATRON What have you been doing?

BROWN Nothing.

MATRON And what do you want to do?

BROWN Nothing.

MATRON Now really, Mr Brown, this won't do, you know.

BROWN Why not?

MATRON You mustn't lose interest in life.

BROWN I was never very interested in the first place.

MATRON Wouldn't you like to get up for a while? Have a walk in the garden? There's no reason why you shouldn't.

BROWN No, I suppose not. But I didn't come here for that. I must have walked thousands of miles, in my time.

MATRON It's not healthy to stay in bed all day.

BROWN Perhaps I'll *get* something.

MATRON Well, isn't there anything you could do indoors?

BROWN What do the other patients do?

MATRON The other patients are here because they are not well.

BROWN I thought patients did things ... *(vaguely)* Raffiawork ...

MATRON Does that appeal to you?

BROWN No.

MATRON I suppose you wouldn't like to make paper flowers?

BROWN What on earth for? You've got lots of real ones.

MATRON *You* haven't got any.

BROWN Well, no one knows I'm here.

MATRON Then you must tell somebody.

BROWN I don't want them to know.

MATRON Who?

BROWN Everybody.

MATRON You'll soon get tired of sitting in bed.

BROWN Then I'll sit by the window. I'm easily pleased.

MATRON I can't let you just languish away in here. You must do *something.*

BROWN *(sighs)* All right. What?

MATRON We've got basket-weaving . . .?

BROWN Then I'll be left alone, will I?

Scene 7 *(The hospital office. The doctor is on the phone.)*

DOCTOR Well, *I* don't know – how many John Browns *are* there in Somerset House? . . . Good grief! . . . Of course, if it's any consolation it may not be his real name . . . I know it doesn't help . . . That's an idea, yes . . . His fingerprints . . . No, no, I'll get them on a glass or something – Well, he might have been in trouble some time. . . .

Scene 8 *(Brown's ward. Brown is working on a shapeless piece of basketry. Matron enters.)*

MATRON What is it?

BROWN Basketwork.

MATRON But what is it for?

BROWN Therapy.

MATRON You're making fun of me.

BROWN It is functional on one level only. If that. *You'd* like me to make a sort of laundry basket and lower myself in it out of the window. That would be functional on *two* levels. At least. *(Regards the mess sadly)* And I'm not even blind. Ladies and gentlemen – a failure! Now I suppose you'll start asking me questions again.

(Matron silently dispossesses Brown of his basketry.)

MATRON What about *painting,* Mr Brown?

(That strikes a chord.)

BROWN Painting ... I used to do a bit of painting.

MATRON Splendid. Would you do some for me?

BROWN Paint in here?

MATRON Nurse Coates will bring you materials.

BROWN What colours do you like?

MATRON I like all colours. Just paint what you fancy. Paint scenes from your own life.

BROWN Clever! Should I paint my last place of employment?

MATRON I'm trying to help you.

BROWN I'm sorry. I know you are. But I don't need help. Everything's fine for me. *(Pause)* Would you like me to paint English countryside?

MATRON Yes, that would be nice.

Scene 9 *(The hospital office. The doctor is on the phone.)*

DOCTOR No ... well, we haven't got anything against him really. He's not doing any *harm.* No, he pays regularly. We can't really refuse ... He's got lots left ...

Scene 10 *(Brown's ward. Brown is painting English countryside all over one wall. He hasn't got very far but one sees the beginnings of a simple pastoral panorama, competent but amateurish. Maggie enters, carrying cut flowers in a vase.)*

MAGGIE Hello – *(She notices)*

BROWN I'll need some more paint.

MAGGIE *(horrified)* Brownie! I gave you drawing paper!

BROWN I like space. I like the big sweep – the contours of hills all flowing – I don't paint leaves, I make you see trees in clumps of green.

MAGGIE Matron will have a fit.

BROWN What are the flowers?

MAGGIE You don't deserve them.

BROWN Who are they from?

MAGGIE Me.

BROWN Maggie!

MAGGIE I didn't buy them.

BROWN Pinched them?

MAGGIE Picked them.

BROWN A lovely thought. Put them over there. I should bring *you* flowers.

MAGGIE I'm not ill.

BROWN Nor am I. Do you like it?

MAGGIE Very pretty.

BROWN I'm only doing it to please matron really. I could do with a bigger brush. There's more paint, is there? I'll need a lot of blue. It's going to be summer in here.

MAGGIE It's summer outside. Isn't that good enough for you?

(Brown stares out of the window: gardens, flowers, trees, hills.)

BROWN I couldn't stay out there. You don't get the benefits.

MAGGIE *(leaving)* I'll have to tell matron, you know.

BROWN You don't get the looking after. And the privacy. *(He considers.)* I'll have to take the curtains down.

Scene 11 *(The hospital office.)*

MATRON It's not as if he was psychotic.

DOCTOR Or Picasso.

MATRON What did the psychiatrist think?

DOCTOR He likes it.

MATRON About *him.*

DOCTOR He likes him too.

MATRON *(sour)* He's likeable.

DOCTOR He knows what he's doing.

MATRON Hiding.

DOCTOR From what? ... *(Thoughtfully)* I just thought I'd let him stay the night. I wanted to go back to bed and it seemed the easiest thing to do. I thought that in the morning ... Well, I'm not sure what I thought would happen in the morning.

MATRON He's not simple – he's giving nothing away. Not even to Nurse Coates.

DOCTOR Well, keep her at it.

MATRON She doesn't need much keeping.

Scene 12 *(Brown's ward. Brown has painted a whole wall and is working on a second one. Maggie sits on the bed.)*

MAGGIE That was when I started nursing, after that.

BROWN Funny. I would have thought your childhood was all to do with ponies and big stone-floored kitchens . . .

MAGGIE Goes to show. What was your childhood like?

BROWN Young . . . I wish I had more money.

MAGGIE You've got a lot. You must have had a good job . . .?

BROWN Centre-forward for Arsenal.

MAGGIE You're not fair! You don't give me anything in return.

BROWN This painting's for you, Maggie . . . If I'd got four times as much money, I'd take four rooms and paint one for each season. But I've only got money for the summer.

MAGGIE What will you do when it's gone?

BROWN *(seriously)* I don't know. Perhaps I'll get ill and have to go to hospital. But I'll miss you, Maggie.

MAGGIE If you had someone to look after you you wouldn't have this trouble.

BROWN What trouble?

MAGGIE If you had someone to cook your meals and do your laundry you'd be all right, wouldn't you?

BROWN It's the things that go with it.

MAGGIE You should have got married. I bet you had chances.

BROWN Perhaps.

MAGGIE It's not too late.

BROWN You don't think so?

MAGGIE You're attractive.

BROWN *(pause)* What are you like when you're not wearing your uniform?

MAGGIE *(saucy)* Mr Brown!

BROWN *(innocent, angry)* I didn't mean –!

MAGGIE *(regretful)* Oh, I'm sorry. . . .

BROWN *(calm)* I can't think of you not being a nurse. It belongs to another world I'm not part of any more.

MAGGIE What have you got about hospitals?

BROWN A hospital is a very dependable place. Anything could be going on outside. Since I've been in here – there could be a war on, and for once it's got nothing to do with me. I don't even know about it. Fire, flood and misery of all kinds, across the world or over the hill, it can all go on, but this is a private ward; I'm paying for it. *(Pause)* There's one thing that's always impressed me about hospitals – they've all got their own generators. In case of power cuts. And water tanks. I mean, a hospital can carry on, set loose from the world. The meals come in on trays, on the dot – the dust never settles before it's wiped – clean laundry at the appointed time – the matron does her round and temperatures are taken; pulses too, taken in pure conditions, not affected by anything outside. You need never know anything, it doesn't touch you.

MAGGIE That's not true, Brownie.

BROWN I know it's not.

MAGGIE Then you shouldn't try and make it true.

BROWN I know I shouldn't.

(Pause)

MAGGIE Is that all there is to it, then?

BROWN You've still got theories?

MAGGIE There's a new one. You're a retired forger.

BROWN Ha! The money's real enough.

MAGGIE I know.

BROWN How do you know?

MAGGIE *(shamefaced)* They had it checked.

(Brown laughs.)

BROWN They've got to make it difficult. I've got to be a crook or a lunatic.

MAGGIE Then why don't you tell them where you came from?

BROWN They want to pass me on. But they don't know who to, or where. I'm happy here.

MAGGIE Haven't you been happy anywhere else?

BROWN Yes. I had a good four years of it once.

MAGGIE In hospital?

BROWN No, that was abroad.

MAGGIE Where have you been?

BROWN All over. I've been among French, Germans, Greeks, Turks, Arabs. . . .

MAGGIE What were you doing?

BROWN Different things in different places. *(Smiles)* I was painting in France.

MAGGIE An artist?

BROWN Oh very. Green and brown. I could turn a row of tanks into a leafy hedgerow. Not literally. Worse luck.

Scene 13 *(The hospital office. The doctor is on the phone.)*

DOCTOR ... He meant camouflage ... Well, I realise that, but there are a number of points to narrow the field ... His age, for one thing. I *know* they were all the same age ... Must be records of some kind .. Service in France and Germany, probably Cyprus, Middle East – Aden possibly ...

Scene 14 *(Brown's ward. Brown has painted two walls and is working on a third.)*

MAGGIE It's very nice, Brownie. Perhaps you'll be famous and people will come here to see your mural.

BROWN I wouldn't let them in.

MAGGIE After you're dead. In a hundred years.

BROWN Yes, they could come in then.

MAGGIE What will you do when you've finished the room?

BROWN Go back to bed and pick up the threads of my old life. It'll be nice in here. Hospital routine in a pastoral setting. That's kind of perfection, really.

MAGGIE You could have put your bed in the garden.

BROWN What's the date?

MAGGIE The 27th.

BROWN I've lasted well, haven't I?

MAGGIE How old are you?

BROWN Twice your age.

MAGGIE Forty-four?

BROWN And more. *(Looking close)* What are you thinking?

MAGGIE Only thinking.

BROWN Yes?

MAGGIE Before I was born, you were in the war.

BROWN *(moves)* Yes. Private Brown.

MAGGIE Was it awful being in the war?

BROWN I didn't like the first bit. But in the end it was very nice.

MAGGIE What happened to you?

BROWN I got taken prisoner.

MAGGIE Oh. Well, you're still private, aren't you, Brownie?

BROWN Better than being dead.

MAGGIE Being private?

BROWN A prisoner. ... Four years.

MAGGIE Is that where you were happy?

BROWN Yes. . . . Funny thing, that camp. Up to then it was all terrible. Chaos – all the pins must have fallen off the map. The queue on the beach – dive bombers and bullets. Oh dear, yes. The camp was like breathing out for the first time in months. I couldn't believe it. It was like winning, being captured. Well, it gets different people in different ways. Some couldn't stand it and some went by the book – yes, it's a duty to escape. They were digging like ferrets. They had a hole out of my hut right into the pines. There were twenty in the hut and I watched all nineteen of them go off. They were all back in a week except one who was dead. I didn't care what they called me, I'd won. The war was still going on but I wasn't going to it any more. They gave us food, life was regulated, in a box of earth and wire and sky, and sometimes you'd hear an aeroplane miles up, but it couldn't touch you. On my second day I knew what it reminded me of.

MAGGIE What?

BROWN Here. It reminded me of here.

Scene 15 *(The hospital office. Present are the doctor, matron and Maggie. The doctor is holding a big book – a ledger of admissions, his finger on a line.)*

DOCTOR John Brown. And an address. *(Looks up)* It was obvious. *(To Maggie)* Well done.

MAGGIE *(troubled)* But does it make any difference?

MATRON What was he doing round here?

DOCTOR Staying with relatives – or holiday, we can find out.

MAGGIE So long ago?

DOCTOR Compound fracture – car accident. The driver paid for him . . . Well, something to go on at last!

MAGGIE But he hasn't done anything wrong, has he?

Scene 16 *(Brown's ward. The painting nearly covers the walls. Brown is finishing it off in one corner.)*

BROWN I was a Regular, you see, and peace didn't match up to the war I'd had. There was too much going on.

MAGGIE So what did you do then?

BROWN This and that. Didn't fancy a lot. I thought I'd like to be a lighthouse keeper but it didn't work out. Didn't like the company.

MAGGIE Company?

BROWN There were three of us.

MAGGIE Oh.

BROWN Then I thought I'd be a sort of monk, but they wouldn't have me because I didn't believe, didn't believe enough for their purposes. I asked them to let me stay without being a proper monk but they weren't having any of that. . . . What I need is a sort of monastery for agnostics.

MAGGIE Like a hospital for the healthy.

BROWN That's it.

MAGGIE *(exasperated)* Brownie!

(He paints.)

BROWN Shouldn't you be working, or something?

MAGGIE I'll go if you like.

BROWN I like you being here. Just wondered.

MAGGIE Wondered what?

BROWN I'm telling you about myself, aren't I? I shouldn't put you in that position – if they find out they'll blame you for not passing it on.

MAGGIE But you haven't done anything wrong, have you, Brownie?

BROWN Is that what you're here for?

MAGGIE No.

(Brown finishes off the painting and stands back.)

BROWN There.

MAGGIE It's lovely.

BROWN Yes. Quite good. It'll be nice, to sit here inside my painting. I'll enjoy that.

Scene 17 *(The hospital office. The doctor is on the phone.)*

DOCTOR . . . Brown. John Brown – yes, he was here before, a long time ago – we've got him in the records – Mmm – and an address. We'll start checking . . . there must be *somebody*. . . .

Scene 18 *(Brown's ward. The walls are covered with paintings. Brown is sitting on the bed. The door opens and a strange nurse – Nurse Jones – enters with Brown's lunch on a tray.)*

JONES Are you ready for lunch –?

(Sees the painting)

My, my, aren't you clever – it's better than anyone would have thought.

BROWN Where's Maggie?

JONES Nurse Coates? I don't know.

BROWN But – she's my nurse.

JONES Yours? Well, she's everybody's.

BROWN *(worried)* You don't understand – she's looking after *me,* you see.

(The doctor enters; Nurse Jones leaves.)

DOCTOR *(cheerful)* Well, Mr Brown – good news!

BROWN *(wary)* Yes?

DOCTOR You're going to have visitors.

BROWN Visitors?

DOCTOR Your sister Mabel and her husband. They were amazed to hear from you.

BROWN They didn't hear from *me.*

DOCTOR They're travelling up tomorrow. All your friends had been wondering where you'd got to –

BROWN *(getting more peevish)* What friends?

DOCTOR Well, there's an old army friend, isn't there – what's his name –?

BROWN I don't know. Where's Nurse Coates gone?

DOCTOR Nowhere. She's round about. I think she's on nights downstairs this week. I understand that you were here once before – as a child.

BROWN Yes.

DOCTOR You *are* a dark horse, aren't you? To tell you quite frankly, we did wonder about you – some quite romantic ideas, not entirely creditable either –

BROWN I told you – I told you there was nothing like that – Why couldn't you –?

DOCTOR Your brother-in-law said something about a job, thought you might be interested.

BROWN *(angrily)* You couldn't leave well alone, could you?

DOCTOR *(pause; not phoney any more)* It's not enough, Mr Brown. You've got to ... *connect. ...*

Scene 19 *(The hospital office. Brown appears, dressed, carrying his bags, from the direction of his room. He sees Maggie and stops. She sees him.)*

MAGGIE Brownie! Where are you going?

BROWN Back.

MAGGIE Back where?

(He does not answer.)

You've got nothing to run for, have you. Nothing to hide. I *know* you haven't.

BROWN I know you know. They've been busy ... I wasn't worth the trouble, you know.

MAGGIE You blame me.

BROWN No. No, I don't, *really*. You had to tell them, didn't you?

MAGGIE I'm sorry – I –

BROWN You thought it was for the best.

MAGGIE Yes, I did. I still do. It's not good for you, what you're doing.

BROWN How do you know? – *you* mean it wouldn't be good for *you*. How do you know what's good for me?

MAGGIE They're coming tomorrow. Family, friends; isn't that good?

BROWN I could have found them, if I'd wanted. I didn't come here for that. *(Comes up to her)* They won. *(Looks out through front doors)* I feel I should breathe in before going out there.

MAGGIE I can't let you go, Brownie.

BROWN *(gently mocking)* Regulations?

MAGGIE I can't.

BROWN I'm free to come and go. I'm paying.

MAGGIE I know – but it *is* a hospital.

BROWN *(smiles briefly)* I'm not ill. Don't wake the doctor, he doesn't like being woken. *(Moves)* Don't be sorry – I had a good time here with you. Do you think they'll leave my painting?

MAGGIE Brownie ...

BROWN Trouble is, I've always been so *well*. If I'd been *sick* I would have been all right.

(He goes out into the night.)

Biographical Notes

Tom Stoppard was born on July 3, 1937 in Czechoslovakia, the son of Eugene Straussler. In 1939 his family moved to Singapore. Before the Japanese invasion in 1942 the family was evacuated to India and his father, who remained behind, was killed. His mother married Kenneth Stoppard, a soldier in the British Army in India. From 1954 to 1960 Tom Stoppard was employed by British papers as a news reporter and theatre and film critic. In 1960 he finished his first play, "A Walk on the Water", later re-titled "Enter a Free Man". During the following years he was a free-lance journalist and drama critic. He was commissioned to write short plays and episodes for radio serials. After the broadcast of several of his plays on TV, including "A Separate Peace", which was televised in 1966, his first world-wide success was the production of "Rosencrantz and Guildenstern are Dead" (1967), a comedy about Hamlet's friends who find themselves in the situation of having the commission to spy on Hamlet and take him to England without knowing at all what is really going on at the Danish Court. To the present day Stoppard has written a considerable number of plays, among which the most important are "Jumpers" (1972), "Travesties" (1974) and "Night and Day" (1978). Stoppard's plays combine serious topics with comedy. Grotesque situations are sometimes presented through a fireworks of verbal wit. He himself confesses to having been influenced by the comedies of Oscar Wilde. Stoppard is widely considered the leading contemporary British comedy writer.

Annotations

5 1 **nursing home** privately owned hospital – **reception counter** desk where incoming patients are registered – 2 **to pull up** to come to a stop – 3 **biggish** rather big – 4 **implacable** [ɪmˈplækəbl] *here:* resolute, firm – **nondescript** [ˈnɒndɪskrɪpt] ordinary looking – 5 **zipped grip** *(A.E.)* bag opened or closed by means of a zip-fastener – 12 **to shuffle** to move or push one over the other – 18 **realisation** realising what it means – 19 **to knock up a taxi** to find a taxi – 26 **aggrieved** hurt in one's feelings – 27 **to sign in** to leave one's name and address with the receptionist

6 1 **privacy** state of being undisturbed, secluded – 2 **to be after s.th.** to want s.th. badly – **a thought strikes him** he suddenly has an idea – 7 **admission** [ədˈmɪʃn] being allowed to enter or stay – 8 **genuine** [ˈdʒenjʊɪn] true – **authority** right given to s.o. (in this case the right to admit new patients); power, the right to command – 13 **flatly** directly – 14 **wary** [ˈweərɪ] cautious – 15 **chit** form to be filled in – **to abide by** [ə'baɪd] to obey – 19 **to jam** to get stuck – 20 **to recoil** to draw back in pain – 21 **dishevelled** [dɪ'ʃevld] with the hair in disorder – **to rouse s.o.** [raʊz] to wake s.o. up – 26 **guardedly** cautiously

7 11 **connection** train due to leave after the arrival of another train – 13 **nuisance** ['nju:sns] a troublesome person – 20 **to make an entry** *here:* to put s.o. on the list of patients and state for what purpose he is admitted – 28 **ward** [wɔ:d] room in a hospital – 33 **picture window** a large window with an attractive view – 35 **to peer** to look closely

8 1 **drive** private road through a park or a garden – 8 **to be put out** to be offended – 19 **matron** ['meɪtrən] woman in charge of the nursing staff of a hospital – 26 **Elastoplast** sticking-plaster – 28 **A1** first class – 32 **to administer** [əd'mɪnɪstə] to put on – 33 **the healing touch** ability to heal

9 14 **to be keen on** to be very interested in – 22 **warm** *here:* friendly – 24 **to bring s.th. off** to succeed in doing s.th. – 26 **disapproval** *here:* negative opinion – 27 **decent** ['di:snt] respectable – 29 **certifiable** [ˌsɜ:tɪ'faɪəbl] *here:* insane – 31 **I got something (there)** there is some truth in what I say – 32 **fuss** *(coll.)* confusion – 33 **to leave well alone** not to mind other people's business – 34 **I'm paying my way** I pay for everything I need

10 5 **passing trade** customers who are attracted into a shop by the window display – 17 **equable** ['ekwəbl] friendly and patient – 26 **lie-in** staying in bed longer than usual – 30 **complaint** illness, disease; grounds for dissatisfaction – 31 **full marks** everything is perfect – 37 **that's not the point** that's not what really matters

11 3 **approach** method of doing something – **straightforward** sincere, honest – **malingerer** [mə'lɪŋgərə] person who *pretends* to be ill – 4 **hypochondriac** [ˌhaɪpə'kɒndrɪæk] person who *thinks himself* to be ill – 5 **on their own terms** the way they are, as such – 16 **to tease s.o.** to make fun of s.o. playfully – 19 **guinea** ['gɪnɪ] formerly 21 shillings (£ 1.05) – 21 **a different kettle of fish** a completely different thing – 23 **to be at s.th.** to intend to do s.th. – 26 **to be cut out for s.th.** to be made for s.th. – 27 **vocation** feeling that one is called to do a certain kind of work – **to transfer** [træns'fɜ:] *here:* to move to another hospital

12 3 **self-sufficient** [sə'fɪʃnt] needing no help from others – 9 **to scan** [skæn] to look at attentively – 23 **embezzler** [ɪm'bezlə] a person who steals money placed in his care – 27 **dignitary** ['dɪgnɪtərɪ] person holding a high office – 28 **charlady** ['tʃɑ:ˌleɪdɪ] woman whose job it is to clean houses, hospitals, etc. – **trolley** a table on small wheels for serving food – 29 **stretcher** a covered framework on which a sick person can be carried – 30 **staffed** equipped with personnel – 31 **to tick someone off** to put a small mark against names in a list – **rota** list of persons who are to do things in turn – 32 **on the run** running away

from the police etc. - 34 **fixation** *(in psychology)* abnormal feeling about, or love for, s.o. or s.th.

13 17 **to be taken aback** to be surprised - 37 **raffiawork** ['ræfɪə] making baskets, hats, etc. from straw

14 11 **to languish away** ['læŋgwɪʃ] to lose health and strength - 16 **Somerset House** births, marriages and deaths used to be registered at Somerset House - 17 **good grief!** *(exclamation of surprise)* - **consolation** comfort, relief - 26 **therapy** ['θerəpɪ] - 29 **laundry** ['lɔ:ndrɪ] washing - 33 **to dispossess s.o. of s.th.** to take s.th. away from s.o.

15 2 **to strike a chord** [kɔ:d] to call up memories - 8 **to fancy** to like - 20 **pastoral** ['pɑ:stərəl] having to do with country life - 21 **competent** ['kɒmpɪtənt] adequate, satisfactory - **amateurish** [ˌæmə'tɜ:rɪʃ] - 26 **big sweep** long, strong strokes with the brush - **contour** ['kɒntʊə] outline or shape of s.th. - 27 **clump** *here:* large mass of paint - 28 **to have a fit** to have a nervous breakdown

16 2 **to pinch** *(coll.)* to steal - 13 **benefit** ['benɪfɪt] advantage - 24 **sour** [saʊə] bad-tempered

17 6 **goes to show** *here:* it shows that one can be mistaken in s.o. - 9 **centre-forward** *(Mittelstürmer)* - **Arsenal** ['ɑ:sənl] traditional London football-club - 29 **saucy** ['sɔ:sɪ] cheeky, coquettish - 35 **dependable** [dɪ'pendəbl] that can be trusted

18 2 **power cut** a breakdown of the electricity system - 3 **on the dot** at the proper time - 4 **appointed** fixed - 13 **Is that all there is to it?** is there nothing more behind it? - 15 **retired** having stopped working, usually because of old age - **forger** person who illegally prints banknotes - 19 **shamefaced** *here:* ashamed - 21 **crook** [krʊk] criminal - **lunatic** ['lu:nətɪk] mad person - 36 **tank** heavy fighting vehicle *(Panzer)* - 37 **leafy** covered with leaves - **hedgerow** ['hedʒrəʊ] row of bushes - **literally** *here:* really - **Worse luck.** too bad.

19 2 **camouflage** ['kæməflɑ:ʒ] the use of paint etc. to hide military vehicles - 3 **to narrow the field** to limit the range of possibilities - 9 **mural** ['mjʊərəl] a wall-painting - 14 **to pick up the threads of one's old life** [θred] to take up one's old life again - 28 **private** ordinary soldier without rank

20 3 **dive bomber** ['daɪvbɒmə] aircraft dropping bombs while diving steeply towards a target - 4 **bullet** ['bʊlɪt] piece of metal fired from a gun - 6 **captured** ['kæptʃəd] taken prisoner - 7 **to go by the book** to stick to the rules - 8 **ferret** ['ferɪt] small animal like a weasel *(Frettchen)* - **pine** *(Kiefer, Pinie)* - 18 **ledger of admissions** ['ledʒə] book in which all admissions are recorded - 26 **compound fracture** [ˌkɒmpaʊnd'frækʧə] breaking of a bone complicated by an open wound - 31 **Regular** soldier of the regular army (as opposed to guerillas) - **to match up to** to be equal to

21 2 **to fancy** to have a liking for - 9 **they weren't having any of that** they didn't accept that - 10 **monastery** ['mɒnəstrɪ] house in which monks live - **agnostic**

[æg'nɒstɪk] one who believes that nothing can be known about God – 13 **exasperated** [ɪg'zɑːspəreɪtɪd] angry, irritated – 20 **to pass s.th. on** to give information to s.o. else – 31 **in the records** on the list of names

22 22 **peevish** bad-tempered – 25 **on nights** on night duty – 28 **a dark horse** person who does s.th. clever or successful when no one expected him to do so – 29 **creditable** ['kredɪtəbl] favourable – 36 **phoney** ['fəʊnɪ] insincere

23 23 **to mock s.o.** to tease, to make fun of s.o.

Interpretation

First Unit: Action and Scenic Structure

1. Is it possible to divide the play into sections? One may follow the division into 19 scenes given by the author or try to establish sections of the plot which are consistent in themselves: the first possibility follows the development of the play in its single scenic steps, whereas the second requires a previous reading of the play as a whole and, on this basis, leads to a division into parts which consist of the important lines of action. In this case one can achieve an order within the play which differs considerably from the original scene sequence.

2. Try to give a scene-by-scene summary of the play. (Note: It largely depends on the reading abilities and the intellectual standard of the pupils whether the discussion of the action and the scenic structure can be dealt with in one teaching unit. For the interpretation of the play it is certainly necessary to gain a complete knowledge of the contents – therefore it is expedient to spend two sessions rather than one on action and scenic structure.)

Scene 1: Brown arrives at a private hospital and wishes to sign in as one would in an hotel. It turns out that he is not ill at all. His perseverance finally wins and the doctor agrees to put him up for a night to avoid trouble.

Scene 2: Brown asks about the hospital regulations. During his dialogue with the nurse it turns out that he has a suitcase full of money on him – it seems that he is planning to stay for a long time. On the other hand, the money and his strange desire to seek seclusion in a private ward without being ill give rise to the suspicion that he has committed a crime. *(Note: The nurse's discovery is a fact which can be seen in its proper relation to Brown's behaviour only on the basis of a knowledge of the complete play: we know that Brown intends to pay for his privacy, but after the first two scenes we can only speculate as to the meaning of the money.)*

Scene 3: The doctor talking to somebody on the telephone. It appears that he is trying to find out about Brown's money and about his identity.

Scene 4: Brown in his ward talking with Maggie and the matron. *(Note: Here we are confronted with the difficulty of whether to concentrate merely on the action or talk about the contents of the various dialogues. As these illustrate Brown's character and his motives and are vital for the overall interpretation of the play, it is suggested that we give detailed summaries of the contents in the respective units.)* Maggie and the matron are unable to grasp Brown's intentions: their viewpoint is that of the hospital. When somebody goes to a hospital he is expected to have some ailment.

Scene 5: The doctor talking on the phone: he is at a loss as to Brown's intentions and is thinking of ways to make him leave the hospital.

Scene 6: Brown is getting on quite well with Maggie. In fact, a friendship develops between the two. She tells Brown about the theories the personnel of the hospital have about him. The matron talks with Brown about an occupation for him.

Scene 7: The doctor on the phone trying to find out Brown's identity.

Scene 8: Brown doing basket-weaving. It turns out that he is rather keen on painting.

Scene 9: This scene shows the doctor's willingness to keep Brown as long as he can pay.

Scene 10: Brown doesn't paint on paper but on the walls of his room. He wants to have his room completely shut off from the outer world.

Scene 11: The doctor and the matron talk about Brown – the confusion his arrival has caused. It seems that the doctor is using Maggie to get further details about Brown's background.

Scene 12: Brown and Maggie talk about his reasons for locking himself up in a hospital. Brown mentions his service in the army in France.

Scene 13: Another attempt on the part of the doctor to find out Brown's identity on the basis of the information given by Brown in the previous scene.

Scene 14: Brown talking about his life as a soldier and a prisoner of war. At the end of the scene he gives Maggie the important information that he has been to this hospital before.

Scene 15: With this information the doctor manages to find out Brown's identity.

Scene 16: The conversation begun in scene 14 is continued. Brown's previous vain attempts to find seclusion and privacy.

Scene 17: Now that the doctor knows who Brown is he starts looking for his relatives.
Scene 18: The doctor announces the imminent arrival of Brown's sister and her husband.
Scene 19: Brown's privacy is disturbed and he is forced to leave the hospital.

Homework

Give a summary of the play.

3. Is there another possibility of subdividing the play?
a) The first two scenes establish the starting-point and the resulting situation: Brown's wish to enter a private hospital and stay there without being ill causes a considerable disturbance among the personnel.
b) From scene 3 onwards we are confronted with an alternating pattern of scenic structure: Brown's dialogues with Maggie – dialogues which serve to give us the necessary information to judge Brown's character and motives – are constantly interrupted by scenes showing the doctor's perplexity and his attempts to get hold of facts concerning Brown's identity.
c) In scene 15 the doctor finds out Brown's identity and in scene 17 he starts locating his relatives. The last three scenes show how the doctor, by trying to make Brown "connect" with reality, drives him out of the hospital.
Now we can see that the alternating pattern of scenes 3 to 16 reflects the basic structure of the contents of the play. There are two antagonistic characters – Brown on the one hand, the doctor on the other – both fighting for their respective positions.

Blackboard

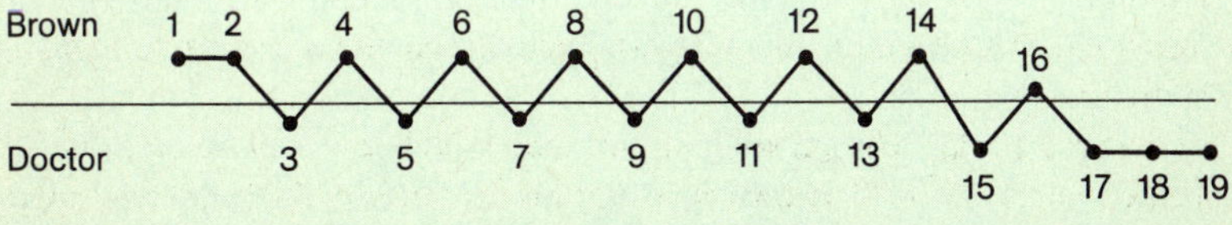

The graphic representation shows that scenes 1 and 2 are fully on Brown's side. Scenes 3 to 17 show the alternating pattern. What is interesting within this pattern is that scenes 4, 6, 8, 10, 12, 14 show Brown obviously holding his position and the doctor (scenes 3, 5, 7, 9, 11, 13) vainly attempting to get the upper hand in this struggle.

Scene 15 marks a turning point: the doctor finds out about Brown. While scene 16 shows Brown still feeling confident, scenes 17, 18, 19 are clearly on the doctor's side, which indicates that he is the winner.

4. Divide the plot into different phases.
Exposition: Brown comes to the hospital; he is described in the stage directions; he states his intention to enter the hospital (scene 1); he settles down and makes himself comfortable (scene 2).
Complication or rising action: The doctor tries to find out about Brown's identity: he wants to turn Brown out of the hospital. There is growing suspense as to whether the doctor will succeed in his attempts (scenes 3–14).
Climax and turning point: Brown's identity has been established (scene 15). There is some overlapping here, as scene 16 shows Brown still unaware of the fact that the doctor's search has at last been successful.
Falling action: The doctor locates Brown's sister and has arrangements made for a visit. He wants Brown to find a job and to resume a normal life outside the hospital (scenes 17 and 18).
Dénouement or catastrophe: Deprived of the privacy he believed to have found, Brown leaves the hospital (scene 19).

5. What is the effect of the alternating pattern of scenic structure? Brown, in his talks with the nurses and especially with Maggie, gradually gives away more and more information concerning his background. This is reported to the doctor, who is finally enabled to trace Brown's former address and his relatives. In the short scenes in which the doctor is shown, we see his reaction to having got additional details. This alternating pattern with the doctor's reactions to the preceding scene creates a constantly rising suspense, with the audience uncertain as to whether the doctor will succeed in his attempts or whether Brown will manage to remain in his ward.
Example: a) In scene 13 the doctor attempts to find out about Brown through the information about Brown's activities in the war given to Maggie in the previous scene.
b) In scene 15 the doctor's attempts are successful because of Maggie's help: at the end of scene 14 Brown says that his stay in a POW camp reminded him of the hospital he is now in. The doctor scans an old ledger of admissions and finds out that Brown had been in this hospital a long time ago. This serves as a starting-point for further investigations.

6. What is the time structure of the play? Basically, there is a chronology of action though one scene does not lead directly into the next. If we take the line of action of either Brown's talks with Maggie or the doctor's telephone calls we can see that there is no uninterrupted action, we rather are shown short glimpses of Brown's life in the hospital or the doctor's repeated attempts to find out facts about Brown. These two lines of action could even take place simultaneously, i.e. the doctor might be making inquiries on the basis of the information gained on the previous day, while Brown is engaged in a renewed conversation with Maggie.

7. What is the relation between action and speech? (Note: This part of the discussion deals with the fact that the evaluation of Brown's character is based not so much on action but on what he says. It can therefore serve as a transition to the discussion of the characters in the second unit.) In this play there is no *action* in the sense of a line of closely connected events. The contents consist mainly of Brown's dialogues with Maggie and the doctor's phone calls. The play is not so much action as the description of Brown's state of mind. Quite often one can find out about a person's character through his actions. In this play, however, there is only one real action, namely Brown's entering the hospital. The larger part of the information concerning Brown's person and character is given through his talks with Maggie about his background, his feelings, desires and expectations. Therefore a close reading of all these dialogues is necessary if we want to obtain a sound assessment of his character and the play as a whole.

Second Unit: The Characters

1. What are the possibilities of representing characters in a play?
a) As is done in this play, there is the possibility of describing the character in the stage directions. *(Note: The representation of a character on stage is a matter to be dealt with in the unit The Play on Stage.)*
b) We can judge a character by what he says and does.
c) Quite often a character is spoken about by other characters which serves as a means to round out one's picture of him.

2. Who is the principal character of the play and how is he introduced?
John Brown is introduced in the first stage direction. We are given his outer appearance (he is wearing a nondescript suit) and a few facts about his person: calm, pleasant, implacable.

3. Who are the other important characters?
a) The doctor: from the discussion of the contents we know that he is to play the part of Brown's antagonist. Apart from the fact that he is dishevelled

from being roused, nothing is said at all concerning the doctor's appearance in the stage directions. In this play the doctor is merely a functional character, that is, he is meant to provide the protagonist (Brown) the opportunity to develop. In this sense he is a "flat character", he is not shown as an individual and fully developed "round character" (see Glossary); he is simply the snooping representative of society (for further discussion of this aspect see section 11 of this unit).

b) The nurses: among these Maggie plays a prominent part. In the first place she serves as a partner for Brown: in her talks with him we get all the information that we need about Brown's character in order to be able to judge him. On the other hand Maggie passes on the information to the doctor, thereby contributing to the doctor's final triumph; see scenes 11 and 15. *(Note: The moral implications of Maggie's behaviour will be dealt with below.)*

4. Discuss Brown's character in the light of the first scene. At the beginning of the play Brown is a "flat character": his name "John Brown" is most common, his clothes are "nondescript", which means that neither his name nor his clothes give us a hint as to how his character is to be imagined. In the course of the play we can gradually picture Brown as an individual and "round character". Brown's quiet determination to obtain a room in the hospital without even trying to hide the fact that he isn't ill at all, points to a certain degree of obstinacy. He has set his mind on entering the hospital and is determined not to be dissuaded from his purpose. His determination is especially manifest in his (voluntary?) inability to grasp the nurse's or the doctor's arguments and objections. He simply doesn't pay attention to them. *(Note: The various misunderstandings will be dealt with in the third unit.)* Another example of his absolute determination is given at the end of scene 2 (p.9, l.7): as his permanent address he puts down Beechwood Nursing Home!

5. Where does Brown give us a first hint of his motives for going to a hospital? A first hint may lead us to a false assumption (at least it does so with the nurse): the fact that Brown's case is full of money (p.8, l.6) could mean that he is a robber seeking refuge. For hints as to his motives we should turn to his talks with Maggie. In scene 4 (p.9, ll.23–31; p.11, ll.21–27) Brown describes a type of behaviour which by normal standards would be considered outright laziness: not only staying in bed all day long but having one's meals there as well. But in a hospital "it's not only understood – it's expected". Scene 4: laziness; a desire for seclusion, not to be disturbed.

6. *Describe the various aspects of Brown's character as they appear in each scene. (Note: This can also be set as homework.)*
Scene 6, p.12, l.33: Brown has stopped "running", i.e. he has given up taking part in the deadening struggle and competition of everyday life. Desire for quiet; lack of interest in life (p.13, ll.26f).
Scene 10, p.15, ll.26f: This passage seems to be in contrast with his desire to live in seclusion, but it turns out that he means to paint an English landscape on the walls of his room and to live there in a world of make-believe. His painting, after all, only mirrors the real world, which he shuns because it does not offer the "benefits" of care and privacy that he enjoys in the hospital.
Scene 12, p.17, l.35–p.18, l.7: Desire for security, to have nothing to worry about.
Scene 16, p.21, ll.2–3, 7–10: attempts to find ways of getting out of touch with the world. P.21, ll.27f: Brown has finished his painting – a mock-world – and is going to sit inside it: desire to create a world according to his own standards.

7. *Give an over-all picture of Brown's character. (Note: As Brown is clearly the central character we ask at the same time for the central theme).* We see the attempt of a man to break out from his everyday life and to escape from any kind of responsibility, be it in the field of social relationships or of personal matters. He doesn't want to live in a world of social and human connections but simply wants to be cared for without committing himself to any duties. We have to deal with such an escapism basically as a moral problem: his desire to be secluded points to the obvious fact that he doesn't agree with life as it is "out there". But mere escapism doesn't solve his problems. Rather, he should face society and try to change it according to his viewpoints. He knows that his attempts at escape are futile (p.18, ll.8–11), but his obstinacy causes him to try again and again. On the other hand Brown doesn't really want to break out – as a prisoner of war he was the only one who didn't escape, though it was everyone's moral duty to try at least once (p.20, l.7). He felt safe and cared for in the relative security of the POW camp. Life after this is horror to him, for now he is obliged to act and take up responsibilities: "... peace didn't match up to the war I'd had. There was too much going on." (p.20, ll.31f).
In his present attempt to avoid facing the real world, he cleverly takes advantage of society: the institutions of the health system provide him with a place where he can retire. He doesn't intend to break down the system but to use it to its very limits.

Homework

How would you judge a person displaying Brown's behaviour? *(Note: The pupils might arrive at a different, more positive interpretation of Brown's behaviour. This could serve as an additonal point of discussion.)*

8. Why doesn't he behave like an "ordinary malingerer" in order to stay in the hospital? With this question we ask about the reasons for Brown's escapism. There is a strange contradiction in Brown's behaviour. He does not simply want to stay in a National Health hospital, where he could get himself admitted free of charge if he chose to behave like "an ordinary malingerer" (p.11, ll.3f), but insists on staying in this particular nursing home (p.11, ll.29–33). Even here he would be accepted if he only pretended to be ill. But instead he keeps maintaining that there is nothing wrong with him. His reason for wanting to stay in this hospital, then, is his craving for seclusion, peace and privacy, which he can only find here. As Brown tells Maggie, the relatively carefree life in the prison camp reminded him of a previous stay in the Beechwood Nursing Home (p.20, l.16). In scene 15 we learn that Brown had indeed been there as a boy. It now becomes apparent that one of the reasons for Brown's longing is his constant wish for a return to childhood. He wants to be cared for and "nursed", but does not want to assume the role of an adult. Adult matters, such as marriage, belong "to another world I'm not part of any more" (p.17, ll.32f), he informs Maggie in the scene in which she virtually proposes to him. In the light of Brown's war experiences and his present longing for seclusion, the title of the play becomes significant (see Suggestions for further work).

9. Compare the development of the picture we get of Brown's character with that of the picture Brown paints. There is a significant relation between the two: parallel to the rounding out of Brown's personality the picture on the wall is brought to completion. What is important here is the fact that it is Brown himself who presents us with his character and who paints the picture. When both pictures – that of Brown's character and the one on the wall – are completed Brown has to leave the hospital.

10. Are there any comic elements in the play? One can basically distinguish between two types of comic passages:

a) those based on comic situations

b) those based on humorous use of language (dealt with in the next unit).

There is a comic situation at the beginning of the play: the deviation from the general rule that a stay in a hospital is only contemplated on the basis of a serious ailment. The comedy underlying this situation and nearly all the

resulting scenes aims at a particular aspect of the health system, namely the private hospitals, which provide medical care to people who can pay. Brown takes advantage of the system and reduces it to absurdity: he is after privacy which he can pay for but he is a perfectly healthy man. Other examples of deviation from what is normally expected are the reversal of roles implicit in Brown's advice to the doctor to go to bed because he looks tired (p.8, ll.33f) and Brown's answer to the matron's inquiry, "And how are we this morning?" (p.13, l.15). In asking the matron in return how *she* feels, Brown simply refuses to accept the role assigned to him.
The opening situation is reversed at the end of the play. The hospital staff now want him to stay, at least until his relatives arrive, whereas he insists on leaving because, after all, he is not ill.

11. Describe the role of society in the play. Society is obviously represented by the doctor and the nurses who, with the exception of Maggie, meet Brown with utter incomprehension. In their behaviour we find some social criticism which aims at the fact that society doesn't permit anybody to live according to his own rules. Anybody who deviates from the system is finally brought back to it. In this sense the doctor is the representative of society, a man who ceaselessly hunts Brown until he can send him back to his former life: "It's not enough, Mr. Brown. You've got to ... *connect.*" (p.22, ll.36f). Criticism of society in general is uttered by Brown (p.23, ll.16f): society as a whole sets up the rules for the individual – determines "what is good for you" – rules to which the individual has to stick, otherwise he is pushed towards the edge of society. A slight criticism of the system of private hospitals is implied in the fact that the doctor is quite willing to let Brown stay in the hospital as long as he can pay, though this reflects on the doctor's character as well (scene 9). On the whole, however, the doctor does not really come alive as a character in his own right. Throughout the play he remains the representative of anonymous forces, as becomes clear at the end, when Brown refers to the forces that have been opposing him by using the personal pronoun *they:* "They've been busy ... You had to tell them, didn't you? ... They won." (p.23, ll.9, 12, 20).

12. Characterize Maggie's behaviour. Maggie is shown to be in a conflict: she is quickly drawn towards Brown, she genuinely wants to help him. On the other hand she has a responsibility towards the doctor: she passes on the information she gets from Brown, thus betraying him. Her loyalty to the doctor finally wins and she contributes to Brown's being turned out, still convinced, however, that she is acting in Brown's best interest. Maggie is the only character in the play who even comes to a vague understanding of what Brown is after when she suggests that what he is looking for is "a hospital for the healthy" (p.21, l.11).

Homework

Characterize Brown, the doctor and Maggie.
Make a list of all the misunderstandings in the play.

Third Unit: Language

1. Describe the comic passages based on the humorous use of language. There are a number of misunderstandings between Brown and the hospital staff which are basically comical. It is not quite clear whether Brown misunderstands the nurses and the doctor intentionally or involuntarily. At any rate, most of these misunderstandings point to his absolute determination to obtain a room in the hospital and to keep it. They are to a large part due to verbal ambiguities:

Board

intended meaning		**how Brown understands it**
	emergency	
a serious case of illness (p.5, l.22; p.7, l.10)		late in the night (p.5, l.25); Brown missed his train (p.7, l.11)
	private hospital	
offering ill people who can pay a nursing home (p.5, l.32)		a place which provides absolute privacy = seclusion (p.6, ll.1f)
	nursing home	
a small, privately owned hospital (p.6, l.4)		a place where one can obtain care and comfort without necessarily being ill (p.6, l.5)
	authority	
the nurse is not in a position to give Brown permission to enter the hospital (p.6, l.8)		strength of character and personality (p.6, l.9)
	observation	
as an entry in the ledger of admissions: Brown is to be observed by the staff to determine what his illness is (p.7, 1.21)		looking at something and admiring it, such as a landscape (p.7, l.22)

problem/complaint	
related to the state of Brown's health (p.10, l.28, 30)	referring to Brown's living conditions in the hospital (p.10, ll.29, 31)

Brown reacts to the words above in a very personal way: the meanings he gives to the words apply to his present situation and state of mind. His determination does not admit any other way of understanding it.

Homework

Show that most of the verbal comedy of the play is due to ambiguities. Try to clarify the respective notions which cause these misunderstandings.

2. *Are there any other misunderstandings and plays on words?* P.7, ll.14f: The doctor asks Brown whether he tried the pubs in the town, obviously referring to Brown's looking for a room. Brown takes this question to refer to his state of sobriety. A similar misunderstanding is found on p.9, ll.1–3, where Brown thinks that the doctor is referring to his injured finger when he speaks of "your case". The only misunderstanding on the part of the staff is Maggie's mistaken assumption that Brown is interested in her sexually when he asks her what she is like when she is not wearing her uniform (p.17, ll.28–31).
There are also some plays on words in which both Maggie and Brown indulge. At the end of his meditations on meals in bed, Brown remarks, "I'd say I'd got something" (p.9, l.31), meaning, "I had a really good idea". Maggie takes this up with the repartee, "If you'd got something, there wouldn't be all this fuss" ("If you were ill, there wouldn't be any problems"). In the same scene, Brown plays on the double meaning of the words "live" and "home" (p.10, ll.7f, 23–25).

3. *Can you give examples of other comic passages?* P.11, l.37; p.12, ll.2f: The doctor's plan to get Brown out of the hospital is "to bore him out" but that is just what Brown expects! P.12, ll.12f: A situation which is near to paradox: Brown's temperature is quite normal, but if he wants to stay he'll "have to do *better* than that", i.e. his temperature must rise. P.17, l.9: Maggie tries to find out Brown's former employment. As Brown seems to sense this, he gives her a totally unexpected answer. Moreover, if he really had been centre-forward for the famous football club the question of his identity would not have arisen. P.18, l.33–p.19, l.2: He has been "painting in France". Maggie immediately assumes what everybody else would have – "an artist?" –, but it turns out that "he meant camouflage".

4. Characterize the level of speech: What kind of language is used in the play? In the dialogues presented in this play we are confronted with everyday language with many idiomatic phrases and colloquialisms. The following are some characteristic examples of everyday speech as employed in the text of this play:

- contractions like *it's, I'm, I've, we're, can't, there's* etc.
- omission of subject, predicate or object, or other parts of a sentence or an expression: *(Good)* evening (p.5, l.9); *(We)* must abide by the regulations (p.6, l.15); *(I)* caught (p.6, l.24); *(I)* knocked (p.5, l.19); *(The)* zip *(of my case)* stuck (p.6, l.30); *(I'll)* be (p.9, l.5), etc.
- simple sentence structure (p.20, ll.2–14).
- repetition of parts of sentences (p.6, l.18; p.7, l.18; p.12, ll.4f; p.21, l.8; p.22, l.31).
- pauses within sentences represented by three dots or a dash: In this play there are two kinds of pauses represented by dots: a) denoting hesitation, excitement etc. b) during the doctor's phone calls, the doctor's listening to his interlocutor on the phone.
- idiomatic and slang expressions: *knocked up* (p.5, l.19); *A1* (p.8, l.28); *fuss* (p.9, l.32); *different kettle of fish* (p.11, l.21) etc.

5. Why does the author use this kind of language? The everyday language used here gives us the impression of realism, that is, of a situation which could happen today and which is rather creditable. Moreover, we must not forget that the dramatic text is a representation of the performance on stage where living people are talking: in order to achieve a lifelike atmosphere it is necessary to give them an appropriate level of speech.

6. How is the presentation of speech in drama different from that in the novel? Speech in drama is represented directly, which means that there are no formulas like "he said" or "he answered". This points to the fact that we are confronted with a situation directly, that is, the names in the text stand for the characters speaking their respective text on stage. There is no mediating narrator who tells a story or comments on the events. If a passage in the text is to be spoken in a particular way, for example *puzzled* (p.5, l.20) or *aggrieved* (p.5, l.26), there is a hint by the author in the stage direction which is to be realized during the performance.

Blackboard
Show the communication situation of *prose* writing vs. *dramatic* writing:

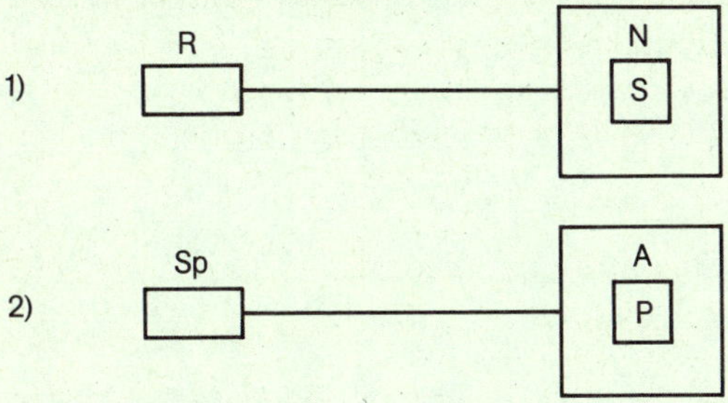

R = reader
N = narrator
S = story
Sp = spectator
A = actor
P = play

We see that in dramatic literature (2) we are confronted with the events of the play, the characters as represented by the actors *directly*, whereas in prose writing (1) the story is usually presented by a narrator.

Fourth Unit: The Play on Stage

1. What are the elements of a dramatic text? The dramatic text consists of two kinds of text:
a) The most important textual element, and the only part of the written text that is conveyed to the audience, is the text to be spoken by the characters themselves, i.e. dialogue and monologue. On the one hand, there is much scope for individual interpretation on the part of the actors, on the other hand, we often find stage directions giving an intimation as to the manner in which a certain passage is to be presented. *(At this point it might be useful to discuss the way a specific scene might be rendered by the actors. Then, bearing this in mind, the scene could be read and recorded by a group of students and compared with the version on the cassette. Differences in interpretation could then be discussed.)*
b) The stage directions constitute the second textual element. They give instructions concerning the stage design, the characters and the way in which certain passages are to be spoken. Thus in the first stage direction of *A Separate Peace* we are given several hints as to the overall situation which have to be followed during the performance: there is a reception counter with a nurse sitting behind it wearing a uniform, we hear the noise of an approaching car, it is 2.30 a.m. Consequently the lights should be quite low, only a dim spot on the nurse etc. Brown is described: it is necessary to have an actor of the right age (later on Brown tells Maggie that he has been a

prisoner of war). He carries his cases which, as we see later on, contain his money, and cause Brown to hurt himself. An important hint is given as to Brown's behaviour at the moment of his entering: he is "quietly pleased", a first expression of his desire to find seclusion and privacy in the hospital. Quite often we find directions concerning the way a character is supposed to express something, e.g. feelings of surprise, of embarrassment etc.

2. What are the elements that go into the staging of a play?

Blackboard

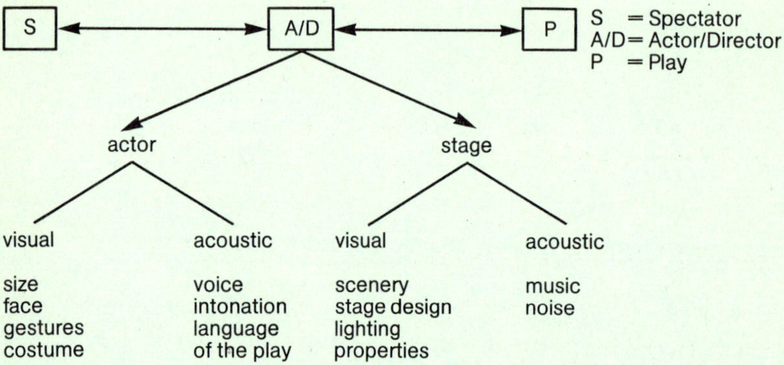

A play, unless it is read, comes into existence in a performance. Thus the actors and the director assume the role of mediators who interpret and visualize the play. In their interpretation A/D must rely both on the primary text and on the stage directions. The play on stage consists of a wide range of visual and acoustic impressions. *(Note: It might be useful to use the above graph and to have the pupils find out the various elements to be used in Stoppard's play.)*

3. What properties do we need? Generally, this information can be taken from the stage directions. Here we need a desk or counter (p.5, ll.1f), a telephone, "two zipped grips" (p.5, l.5), a "bed and the usual furniture" (p.7, ll.28f), which needn't consist of more than a table and chair.

4. How are we to imagine the scenery? The scenery shouldn't be naturalistic in order to make a quick change of scenes possible. For the scenes at the reception desk we simply need the desk with a telephone and a chair. This scenery could be used for the doctor's telephone calls as well. For Brown's ward we need a hospital bed and a table with a vase on it (for the flowers brought by Maggie).

5. How should the staging of the play be carried out? In order to make the alternating scenic structure of the play quite clear we should make it possible to change very quickly from one scene to the next without much moving of stage properties. Therefore we keep both acting areas on stage simultaneously and light them with a sharp limited spot according to the needs of the scenic progression of the play. Now it is quite easy to switch from one place of action to the other. To visualize the progress of Brown's painting one can use several layers of newsprint, each showing the painting in a different stage of completion.

Blackboard:

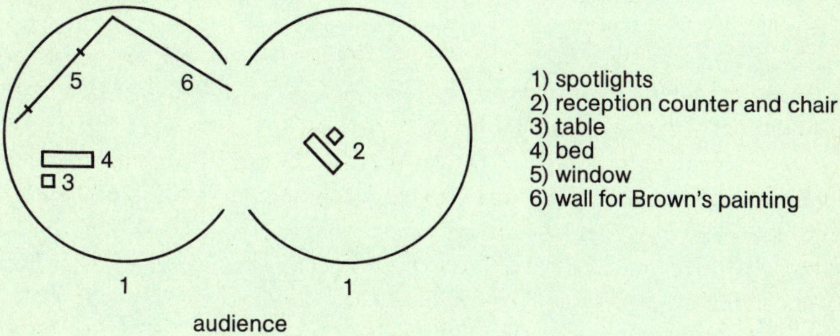

Suggestions for Further Work

1. What does the title of the play suggest? The title "Separate Peace" is taken from politics or warfare meaning that a country makes peace with one of its opponents without having come to terms with the others. *Can this meaning be transferred to the play?* Brown finds himself in a kind of warfare with society, here represented by the doctor and the personnel. Brown wants to make peace but on his own terms, which society, however, cannot accept. The word "separate" is used deliberately by Stoppard: it reflects the fact that Brown asks for "separation" from society, he wants to be left alone to find peace. His warfare with the needs and responsibilities forced upon him by society compels him to make an attempt at separation: he wants to make peace with society by separating himself from it.

2. In the last scene Brown complains to Maggie about his relatives coming to see him. He leaves the hospital with the remark "they won" (p.23, l.20). What does he mean by this? It is possible that Brown thinks of his relationship with society as a kind of warfare: he tries to make his wishes come true and not to succumb to the requirements of society. It seems that *they* not only refers to his sister Mabel and her husband but to the doctor and the nurses as well, to society in general. Tom Stoppard shows Brown's struggle in the hospital as a kind of contest between Brown and the doctor where, at the beginning, Brown is in the lead, but the doctor, who represents society, finally wins.

3. Interpret the following passage:

MAGGIE ... It's not good for you, what you're doing.

BROWN How do you know? – *you* mean it wouldn't be good for *you*. How do you know what's good for me? (p.23, ll.15–17).

One of the central passages of the play: Brown accuses Maggie of setting up standards of behaviour for him. He maintains that she cannot know his reasons for acting as he does and therefore cannot judge him. It is convenient for her to prescribe for him a specific way of behaviour which is the easiest to deal with for her – if Brown sticks to the hospital regulations and behaves as everybody else does he isn't a nuisance to, and doesn't cause problems for, the system. In order to know what is good for Brown she must know Brown's motives very thoroughly. Society, even Maggie who has more sympathy for Brown than anybody else, cannot accept him as he is. As he does not fit into any of the usual categories, something more out of the way has to be found to explain his strange behaviour: he must either be a lunatic (cf. p.11, ll.13–17), a train-robber (p.12, l.19) or a spy from the Ministry (p.12, l.21; cf. ll.23, 25, 34, p.18, l.15).

4. The play as comedy. In this play we find comedy of situation and verbal comedy (see the respective units above). But there is no "happy ending" in the sense that Brown manages to stay or that he starts a relationship with Maggie: Brown is the loser. We find a rather serious subject – a man fighting to live according to his own standards and being forced back into society – treated in a comical way. This manner of dealing with a topic can be found in nearly all of Stoppard's plays.

5. Is there a "touch of the absurd" in this play? (see Glossary). Only in Brown's situation and in his life-style is there to be found a certain touch of the absurd. The form and structure of the play itself are quite traditional: there is clearly a beginning, a middle and an end; there is a strong feeling of suspense as to what will happen next; the motives of the characters can be laid bare to a certain extent. The only "absurd" aspect is Brown's attempt to retreat from the world, to live "set loose from the world" (p.18, l.3). This is a theme dealt with by Samuel Beckett, the most important representative of absurd writing, in his novels *More Pricks Than Kicks* (1934) and *Murphy* (1938).

6. The theme of contradiction. In this play we find contradictions on several levels: a) Brown feels perfectly healthy but wants to retreat to a hospital. b) He must do better (i.e. must become ill) in order to stay in the hospital (p.12, l.13). c) The patient gives medical advice to the doctor (p.8, 11, 33f). d) Brown wants to be secluded from the outside world but he paints a landscape picture on the wall of this room. e) Brown wants a "monastery for agnostics" and a "hospital for the healthy" (p.21, ll.10f). f) A reversal of behaviour pattern: Brown wants to "breathe in" (p.23, l.21) before he leaves the hospital and goes into the open air. g) In this world of contradiction Brown feels his trouble to be his health: sickness comes to mean "happiness" (p.23, ll.31f).
Together with the "camouflage theme" dealt with below the "theme of contradiction" points to Brown's standard of values which is quite contrary to that of society in general: therefore, according to Brown's notions, the following terms come to mean:

happiness – stay in hospital; sickness; loneliness; separation
healthiness – unhappiness; trouble; having to face the world

At the end of the play Brown finally comes to an understanding of this problem: his trouble is that his standard of values and consequently his behaviour patterns do not match with those of society.

7. The camouflage theme. Camouflage means *conceal, hide, deceive.* Brown's task in the war was to camouflage tanks, i.e. to hide something from the eyes of the enemy. Now he himself hides away from society and tries to conceal himself from its demands.

James Saunders

A Slight Accident

There is the sound of a shot. As the curtain rises Penelope is standing, becomingly, with an equivocal expression on her face and a revolver, still smoking, in her hand. At some distance lies the body of a man. Penelope, looking perhaps rather as might a woman of means who had just broken her husband's favourite piece of antique china, looks at the body, without moving towards it, then at the revolver. It continues to smoke. She waves it about, blows down the barrel, coughs, fans away gracefully the trace of gun-smoke still hanging in the air, and considers the situation.

PENELOPE Oh dear ... *(She goes up to the body, peers at it without stooping.)* Harry ... Harry dear, don't be ridiculous ... really, if you can't take a joke ... Will you please get up ... Harry, do get *up* ... Harry! Harry? *(She gently nudges it with her toe.)* Harry?

(No answer. She goes to the telephone, dials, and waits.)

Hallo, Camilla darling. Am I disturbing you? ... You are? Oh ... I wondered if you could come up for a few minutes ... No, I *can't* wait. I've just done something rather tiresome and I need company. Come and watch the rest of the – My husband isn't much company at the moment ... You don't know at *all* what I mean ... Darling, *please* ... Yes, we've had it fixed ... Yes, the picture's perfect now ... That's sweet of you.

(She hangs up, switches on the television, looks at the body again.)

Everything happens to me ...

(She takes another look at the body, goes to the door, turns back as though coming in for the first time.)

Penelope darling – Oh ...

(She hurriedly covers the body with a bearskin rug. She arranges meticulously and with taste several cushions on the rug. The doorbell rings. She goes to answer it. The television comes on as she comes back with Camilla.)

CAMILLA Penelope darling, what *has* happened?

(Penelope says nothing. Her eyes on Penelope, Camilla sits before the

television, and is drawn into it. Penelope walks to and fro, rehearsing her lines.)

ACTRESS 1 I've had this to say for twenty years: you're rotten, you've always been rotten and you always will be rotten.

ACTRESS 2 You despise me ...

ACTRESS 1 You killed my brother. You drove my son to suicide. You ruined my cousin. All you touch you defile.

(Sobs)

ACTRESS 1 You sent my husband mad; you corrupted his nephew.

ACTRESS 2 Why do you hate me?

(Sobs. Sound of door opening)

ACTRESS 1 You're filthy. Filthy.

ACTRESS 2 Philip! Thank God you're safe.

(Sound of door closing)

ACTOR 1 My God I need a drink.

(Sound of door opening)

ACTRESS 1 I'm going to my room.

(Sound of door closing)

ACTRESS 2 Philip, where's ...?

ACTOR 1 Dead.

(Sound of breath being caught)

ACTRESS 2 How ...?

ACTOR 1 Tincture of iodine. Evelyn can't we start afresh? Go away somewhere?

ACTRESS 2 Where?

ACTOR 1 Anywhere. Trucial Oman.

ACTRESS 2 You mean – Together? You're vile. Vile ...

ACTOR 1 You fool. Don't you realise this is your last chance?

ACTRESS 2 I can't take any more, I can't, I can't!!!

(Sobs. Sound of door opening)

ACTRESS 1 I heard a shot.

ACTOR 1 What!

ACTRESS 2 Not ...

(Sound of door opening. Sound of doorbell)

Oh God . . . Vincent!

(Sound of door closing)

ACTOR 2 Quite a pretty picture, isn't it? Well, the time has come.

ACTOR 1 My God I need a drink.

(Sound of telephone)

ACTRESS 1 Don't answer it! It's a trap!

(Sound of door closing. Sound of doorbell)

ACTRESS 2 Look out, he's got a knife!

ACTOR 2 You've had your last drink, you swine!

(Sound of a shot. Sound of breath being caught. Sound of gurgling. Silence. Sound of a glassful of whisky and soda dripping onto a tiled fireplace. Silence. Sound of a body dropping onto the floor.)

ACTRESS 2 He's . . .

ACTOR 1 Dead.

ACTRESS 2 You'd better go.

ACTRESS 1 And leave you . . .?

ACTRESS 2 Yes. Leave me. Go.

(Sound of door closing)

ACTOR 1 Coming, Claire?

(Sound of door opening)

ACTOR 2 You'll be all right?

(Sound of door closing)

ACTRESS 2 I'll be all right. Leave the gun.

(Sound of door closing. Silence. A shot. Silence. Sound of a body falling on to the floor. Music. Camilla looks round at Penelope, arguing with herself. She switches off.)

CAMILLA I'll not watch part two after all.

PENELOPE No?

CAMILLA I don't think so. All the interesting characters are dead already.

PENELOPE That's what I always say.

CAMILLA Where's Harry?

PENELOPE Who?

CAMILLA Your husband . . .

PENELOPE What about him?

CAMILLA Where is he?

PENELOPE Why?

CAMILLA I'm only asking.

PENELOPE Why do you ask, what do you mean, do you think I've murdered him or something, why are you looking at me like that? As a matter of fact he's lying down.

CAMILLA Isn't he well?

PENELOPE No. Yes. I don't know.

CAMILLA You *must* know.

PENELOPE Why must I?

CAMILLA But darling –

PENELOPE I don't live in my husband's pocket. Harry's a free agent; if he wants to be well or unwell he doesn't have to give me an account of it. Do you think I go running around after Harry saying, are you well, Harry, are you still well?

CAMILLA Forget I asked . . .

PENELOPE He wanted to lie down, so he lay down.

CAMILLA All *right,* darling.

(Pause)

So what's the trouble?

(Penelope looks at her.)

You said you'd done something stupid.

PENELOPE I didn't say that at all. I don't know what you mean.

CAMILLA Penelope darling, you rang me up –

PENELOPE I didn't say stupid.

CAMILLA Let's not play with words . . .

PENELOPE Why not, words are important. What do we have to play with but words? I'm not going to have you coming up here at a moment's notice accusing me of being stupid.

CAMILLA Oh, dear . . .

PENELOPE What I said was 'tiresome'. It was an accident.

CAMILLA What was?

PENELOPE To be stupid you have to do it on purpose. It's like breaking the handle off a cup; if you do it on purpose that's stupid but if it's an accident it's tiresome, that's all, certainly not stupid. I didn't do it on purpose ... I don't think ...

CAMILLA You didn't.

PENELOPE Why should I?

CAMILLA But why all this fuss about breaking a handle off a cup?

PENELOPE I haven't broken any handles, darling, it's nothing to do with handles.

CAMILLA I see.

PENELOPE You don't see.

CAMILLA Very true.

(Pause)

Are you going to give me a drink?

(Penelope begins to go through the usual motions.)

I do like your curtains ... Of course, you don't *have* to tell me anything ...

PENELOPE Give me time, darling ... Some things are so silly they're embarrassing. I mean, there's the normal course of events carrying itself along as usual, in a nice straight grey line, and then suddenly out of the blue there's this ludicrous occurrence, spoiling the whole natural sequence. *(She is still busying herself with the drinks.)* I mean, life is full of actions you couldn't possibly explain. Nearly everything we do is – inexplicable. And what difference does it make if the result of a particular action happens to be rather – extreme? ... *(She turns.)* Camilla darling ...

CAMILLA Penelope ... What's that?

PENELOPE What?

CAMILLA That heap.

PENELOPE Heap?

CAMILLA There.

PENELOPE I don't see anything.

CAMILLA It looks like a body covered with a bearskin rug, with cushions for camouflage.

PENELOPE Ridiculous.

CAMILLA May I look?

PENELOPE It's a bearskin rug, there's nothing there, I don't know what you're talking about – I forbid you to touch it! I asked you up because I thought I could rely upon you as a friend.

CAMILLA I'd like to help –

PENELOPE I took you for a woman of delicacy and understanding.

CAMILLA But I don't know what to be understanding *about.*

PENELOPE And all you can do is pry into my life and peer under my carpets as though you expect to find bodies under them all, and then you accuse me of shooting my husband.

CAMILLA Shooting your –?

PENELOPE There you go again!

CAMILLA But I didn't mention –

PENELOPE Then why make these grotesque allusions to a perfectly ordinary rug and a few cushions?

CAMILLA It was a joke, darling –

PENELOPE A joke! You think it's a joke!

CAMILLA As for your husband, I didn't mention your husband. It just looked like an anonymous body, that's all; it could be anyone's husband.

PENELOPE And I suppose you're thinking: ah, I didn't notice the shot because there were shots in the play and I mistook the sound of Penelope shooting her husband for someone in the play getting shot. And now you're trying to think back to whether there was one more shot than there were bodies. You've got it all worked out, haven't you? I daresay you've decided on a motive too. Well, let me inform you that in all the years of our marriage Harry and I have never once quarrelled, not once. Show me another couple you can say that about, give me their names. Harry and I have lived in perfect harmony. *There,* there are the slippers I laid out ready for him, just where he knows he can find them; there is the bunch of flowers he brings me home regularly every single Thursday, for some reason. My God, I do think one could expect at least one's friends to show a little understanding and sympathy and not go leaping to the most bizarre conclusions at every opportunity. Well, it's as they say: you climb in company, but you fall alone, and woe betide you if you expect your closest friend to stretch out a hand to check your descent.

CAMILLA You're not unique, you know.

PENELOPE Hm?

CAMILLA I've never quarrelled with Rodger either. Rodger's never quarrelled in his life; he doesn't believe in it. Rodger thinks one should never raise one's voice after the age of two.

PENELOPE Then you know what I'm talking about.

CAMILLA I know what you're talking about, darling.

PENELOPE Another drink?

CAMILLA Yes please ... May one ask one question?

PENELOPE Hm?

CAMILLA You won't think I'm prying?

PENELOPE Probably.

CAMILLA That is a boot, is it?

PENELOPE Not at all. It's a shoe.

CAMILLA I see.

(Penelope hands her a drink.)

PENELOPE It's been one of those days, you know?

(Pause)

CAMILLA The evenings are drawing in . . .

PENELOPE Darling, you don't have to fill in the pauses.

(Pause)

PENELOPE Language is so limited.

CAMILLA Hm?

PENELOPE Who was that scientist who was once caught, alone in his room, dropping a little bit of cotton wool into a basin, to see whether he could hear it hit the bottom?

(Camilla takes a long look at her.)

Can you imagine him trying to explain himself? Of *course* he knew he wouldn't be able to hear it. He just did it – because he knew it wouldn't work . . . Let me start at the beginning, darling. You see, what happened –

(Door bell. Pause)

CAMILLA Shall I go?

(Penelope nods. Camilla goes; she comes back with Rodger, who is dressed as one might expect a stockbroker's son to be dressed at ten in the evening.)

RODGER I'm *not* following you about, dear; it's just that I'd made the cocoa –

CAMILLA I'm sorry, darling, Rodger's come up.

RODGER You don't have to apologise. How are you, Penelope?

PENELOPE Oh, I'm – first class.

RODGER Jolly good. And Harry?

PENELOPE He's first class.

RODGER Mhm. Well, dear, what are we going to do about the cocoa?

CAMILLA Do we have to do anything about it?

RODGER It's down there getting cold. *(To Penelope)* I go into the kitchen as I do every evening, make the cocoa, take it into the lounge and I find my wife's disappeared. Upset the routine completely.

CAMILLA Go and drink the cocoa if you want to.

RODGER It isn't the cocoa, dear, it's the principle of the thing. Whether I drink the cocoa or not, the routine's been upset; you can't get away from it. I say, what's that?

PENELOPE Nothing.

RODGER Yes, but what is it?

PENELOPE Why is everyone so inquisitive? I invite people up and all they do is poke around asking what's this, what's that? It's an Axminster carpet wrapped up in a bearskin rug.

RODGER But –

PENELOPE The cleaners are calling for it in the morning – the carpet, the rug and the cushions. They all need cleaning.

RODGER Yes, but –

PENELOPE Down the centre of the carpet is a long pole to make it easier to carry the carpet and on the end of the pole is a shoe, so that the person carrying the carpet will not be injured by the end of the pole. The shoe is a safety measure. Now I hope everyone's satisfied.

RODGER There seem to be two shoes.

PENELOPE Then there must be two poles, mustn't there? What will you drink?

RODGER Cocoa. Where's Harry?

PENELOPE Whisky or gin?

RODGER Yes, please. Where's –?

PENELOPE *(pouring a drink)* He's out of town.

RODGER Out of town?

PENELOPE Yes.

RODGER I thought he was in town.

PENELOPE He was in town, now he's out of town.

CAMILLA Not lying down.

RODGER Out of town not lying down?

PENELOPE He's out of town lying down. Is there anything to prevent that?

CAMILLA If he's out of town how do you know he's lying down?

PENELOPE He rang me up.

CAMILLA To say he was lying down.

PENELOPE *Yes.* He rang me up to say he was out of town, and that he was lying down. He was lying down when he rang me up. Do you mind?

CAMILLA Lying down in a telephone box.

PENELOPE No, darling, in a hotel bedroom. He rang me from an out-of-town bedside telephone to say he was lying down.

(Pause)

RODGER Is Harry in the habit of –?

PENELOPE Why are you persecuting me?

CAMILLA It just seems a little unusual . . .

PENELOPE What are you insinuating? That he isn't out of town lying down? That he's in town standing up? Is that what you're getting at?

CAMILLA No, darling . . .

PENELOPE Do you think I have him standing up in a cupboard somewhere? Do you? Do you want to search my cupboards? Really, this is too bad.

(Pause)

RODGER Leeds?

CAMILLA What?

RODGER I was talking to Penelope.

PENELOPE What?

RODGER Leeds?

PENELOPE Leads what?

RODGER The town Leeds.

PENELOPE The town leads what?

RODGER Is it the town Leeds?

PENELOPE Is what the town Leeds?

RODGER Is Harry in the town Leeds?

PENELOPE No.

RODGER He was last year.

PENELOPE Well he isn't this year.

(Pause)

CAMILLA Where then?

PENELOPE Oh . . . Hull.

(Pause)

CAMILLA Why go to Hull to lie down?

PENELOPE I don't want to pursue this subject.

CAMILLA All right, darling.

(Pause)

RODGER Why not?

PENELOPE I just don't.

RODGER Mhm.

PENELOPE He had to go to Hull to see a client.

CAMILLA In a hotel.

PENELOPE In an office, in an office.

RODGER Then they went to the hotel –

PENELOPE Then *he* went to the hotel, since he felt unwell, and lay on the bed and rang me up. Do you want his telephone number as well!

RODGER I could give him a ring –

PENELOPE Well you're not going to. I'm not going to have him pestered by all and sundry when he's not well . . . Poor Harry . . .

RODGER Poor old Harry . . . It's his own fault, of course.

PENELOPE What do you mean?

RODGER Breaking his routine. It leads to trouble. He goes to Hull, a thing he never does; he becomes ill. Naturally. He should have let the client come to London. Let the client be sick.

CAMILLA What are you talking about?

RODGER Look at me. Am I ever ill? No. Why?

CAMILLA Because you haven't the imagination.

RODGER Because I stick to routine. Because I have every action catalogued, right down to the blowing of my nose at set intervals.

PENELOPE Catalogued?

RODGER I keep a book. A sort of manual of running instructions. I've worked it out over the years. What's childhood for if not to learn one's running routine? By the time I was twenty I knew precisely what I'd be doing any minute of the day. It's the only way to live safely. Behind the facade, no, the bastion of habit, of routine, anarchy lurks, waiting to spring . . .

CAMILLA Rodger dear –

RODGER Look at this case in the paper today. A hairdresser's assistant in Balham is working quietly along a row of seven ladies sitting under the hairdriers when suddenly he takes up a pair of scissors and stabs all seven of them one after another. Why did it happen? I'll tell you: he lost respect for routine, he threw his habits over-board. He left the well-ordered terrain of habituality and struck off into the jungle of infinite possibility, where every step is into unknown country. Think of him. I may continue to dry the hair of these women who mean nothing to me, he says to himself. I may go along the line asking are they comfortable and offering them the *Tatler* and *Country Life*; but equally I may not. But if not, what? Indeed, what not?

(Pause)

CAMILLA What are you trying to prove?

RODGER That I'm invulnerable; impregnable; safe.

CAMILLA That you'll never stab a woman with a pair of scissors while she's sitting under a hairdrier.

RODGER Yes, for instance. Tell me, have I ever committed a crime? Ever run anyone over or been run over? Ever missed a train? I'm a creature of habit; I'm as safe as houses.

PENELOPE You shouldn't be too sure.

RODGER Well, here's the proof.

PENELOPE Where?

RODGER Here. Me. I sit here after thirty-nine years without a scar, without a worry, without a stain on my character; I did today what I did yesterday, and I shall do tomorrow what I did today. Nothing went wrong today, nothing can go wrong tomorrow. If I meet the untoward on my way, I shall size it up from a distance, and walk gingerly round it.

CAMILLA What have you got there, Rodger?

(Rodger, in making himself more comfortable in his chair, has removed the hard lump from under his cushion. He stares at it.)

PENELOPE Be careful, Rodger, it may have a hair-trigger.

RODGER It's not loaded, obviously.

PENELOPE D'you want to try it?

(Rodger examines it.)

CAMILLA Loaded?

(He nods.)

PENELOPE You see?

RODGER Isn't it rather dangerous, leaving loaded revolvers lying around?

PENELOPE It isn't leaving them lying around that's dangerous, it's picking them up and pulling the trigger. There you are, you see, the man of habit, sitting drinking gin and tonic with a loaded revolver pointed at your wife.

RODGER The safety catch is on; I do know a little about revolvers.

PENELOPE Do you know how little one finger has to move in order to pull the trigger?

RODGER I tell you the safety catch is on.

PENELOPE Do you know how little the thumb has to move to put it off?

(Rodger smells the barrel.)

RODGER It's been fired.

PENELOPE Has it?

RODGER One shot.

PENELOPE Really?

RODGER Recently.

(Pause)

PENELOPE Yes. That's right. It was me.

RODGER You?

PENELOPE Yes. I pulled the trigger.

CAMILLA When?

PENELOPE This evening. I had it in my hand and the trigger got pulled.

RODGER By you.

PENELOPE Who else?

CAMILLA So there *was* an extra shot.

RODGER During the play. Of course. There was a shot, and no one fell down. It seemed rather strange at the time.

PENELOPE That's what it was, you see.

CAMILLA What were you firing at? Or was it an accident?

PENELOPE More drinks, anyone?

RODGER Of course it was an accident, what else could it have been?

PENELOPE More drinks?

CAMILLA Was it?

PENELOPE What?

CAMILLA An accident?

PENELOPE Now let's see, yours was a gin as well, wasn't it? . . . Yes, of course is was an accident.

CAMILLA You just picked it up and it went off.

PENELOPE I just picked it up and – pulled the trigger.

RODGER By accident.

PENELOPE Naturally . . . That is to say . . .

CAMILLA What?

PENELOPE That is to say, I pulled the *trigger* on purpose. If that's what you mean.

CAMILLA What else could we mean, darling?

RODGER So it *wasn't* an accident.

PENELOPE It *was*.

CAMILLA But you did it deliberately.

PENELOPE I didn't do it deliberately . . . I did it on purpose . . .

CAMILLA *Darling* . . .

PENELOPE Oh, *really* . . . Why are you so *obtuse*? Why do you pretend everything's so *simple*?

CAMILLA There's accident, darling, and there's design, darling –

PENELOPE And there's Rodger sitting there with a glass in his hand, about to raise it to his lips.

RODGER I don't get the drift.

PENELOPE Did you pick it up deliberately?

RODGER Yes ... Well – half deliberately ...

PENELOPE *Half* deliberately; *Rodger* ... You picked it up, on purpose to drink it, without deliberation ... You raise it to your lips, and take a sip, on purpose to drink it, without deliberation. And if the glass contained poison, and by some accident nothing happened to stop you –

RODGER But it doesn't.

PENELOPE Or if it were not a glass of gin and tonic but a revolver, and you didn't raise it to your lips without deliberation but raised it with your finger on the trigger, without deliberation, and somebody said 'Pull it' and you pulled ...

RODGER I don't know what you're talking about.

PENELOPE I picked up the revolver, just as you picked up that glass; I put my finger on the trigger, as one does automatically; I held it up like this, as one does; and ...

RODGER You *pulled* the *trigger.*

PENELOPE – And by some – accident, by some mischance ... nothing happened to stop me ...

(Slight pause)

PENELOPE Of all the thousand and one things that could have happened, nothing did ... Suppose, for instance, there'd been a mouse.

RODGER A mouse?

PENELOPE *A mouse,* yes ...

RODGER You shot at a mouse?

PENELOPE No, Rodger, I didn't shoot at a mouse, but let's say there *was* a mouse; which ran out from under that chair.

RODGER Impossible.

PENELOPE What's impossible about it?

RODGER There are no mice.

PENELOPE How do you know? How do you know what's behind the wainscot?

RODGER If there were mice in this flat, there'd be mice in our flat.

PENELOPE We could have our own private mice, couldn't we?

RODGER No, because they'd have to pass our flat to get here.

PENELOPE Well they did. They came during the day, while you were out. Or watching television. There were mice on television and you thought you were hearing television mice scuttling by, just as with the shot. My finger was on the trigger, when suddenly – out from under that chair, frightened by a cat, ran the mouse.

RODGER Cat! What cat?

PENELOPE A cat, any cat. A cat from downstairs. It came up, attracted by the smell of milk.

RODGER There's no cat downstairs. We have no cat; the Fergusons on the first floor, they have no cat; the Hartleys on the ground floor, they have no cat. Even the porter has no cat. Then whose cat was it?

PENELOPE It was *no one's* cat. It was a stray cat. The town's full of stray cats, wild cats, cats that have never known a proper home. Born in coal cellars and, and bicycle sheds, fending for themselves. It's the old story. They eat what they can; it's a hard life. This one was looking for mice on the stairs.

CAMILLA You said it smelt milk.

PENELOPE It smelt milk and forgot the mice. But when it got up here it smelt mice and forgot the milk. The cat crept behind the chair and the mouse, which had been attracted by the smell of the biscuits I was to have with my milk –

CAMILLA You don't drink milk, Penelope . . .

PENELOPE Camilla, *please* . . . The mouse, alarmed, bounded from under the chair –

RODGER Followed by the cat.

PENELOPE Followed by the cat, and I, surprised, forgot that I'd been about to accidentally, on purpose, without deliberation, pull the trigger, and . . . didn't. That would have been an accident, wouldn't it? So, by the same token, it was an accident that, as you say, we have no mice; no cats. And that's how the unfortunate accident happened. . . .

CAMILLA What accident?

PENELOPE Darlings, I'm forgetting your glasses.

CAMILLA What accident?

(Penelope turns to her; they look at each other for some time.)

Penelope . . .

PENELOPE *Life* – is by no means as straightforward as it's supposed to be.

RODGER If it wasn't a mouse, what *were* you aiming at?

PENELOPE You think we live in the age of reason, don't you? You think we can put our life under the microscope, prod it this way and that way with a little pair of tweezers and say: ah, yes; I did this because of this and this because of this. How simple!

RODGER Penelope, what –?

PENELOPE Ten years ago, on my way to visit a taxidermist, I got stuck in a lift between the fourth and fifth floors.

(Rodger scratches his head.)

Three-quarters of an hour later, coming down, between the fourth floor and the third floor, I got stuck in the same lift, together with the same stranger I was stuck in the lift with on the way up. Improbable? *Yes.* But it happened. That's what caused it ...

RODGER Caused what?

PENELOPE That's how I met Harry. And off went the chain of events on its immutable course. And what d'you think I had to do with it?

RODGER I don't get the drift ...

PENELOPE I mean we *pretend*, Rodger, we *pretend* ... that we're in control, that we decide ... Well maybe we *do*; but what *makes* us decide ...?

RODGER I don't agree with anything you're saying –

PENELOPE Of course you don't; you're not able to. You think we play our lives like fish.

RODGER Yes, like fish –

PENELOPE You think we stand on the banks of the river of life, all dressed up in our oilskins of habit, catching events like salmon as they leap past. It may seem so to you, Rodger; but are the events, in reality, catching us?

RODGER What *were* you aiming at?

(Pause)

PENELOPE Who, me ...?

(Slight pause)

RODGER Of course we're in control; we can choose, can't we?

PENELOPE D'you think I had a *choice* of marrying Harry or not marrying Harry?

RODGER I'm not talking about Harry. I'm talking about life –

PENELOPE I'm talking about Harry. I had no choice.

RODGER Nonsense ...

PENELOPE Of course I had no choice. We met, perforce, in a lift. And there we were later, drinking good coffee after a delicious meal in an expensive restaurant ... It was a foregone conclusion; so much so that he didn't even bother to ask me; he *told* me. We'll get married, he said. Yes, I said, Naturally; of course; what else? Why not? ... A dreadful gypsy violinist scraped his bow plaintively two tables away, while I sipped chartreuse; of course, why not, what else, who could think otherwise ...?

RODGER You could have said no.

PENELOPE Of course I couldn't, how ridiculous.

RODGER I don't see anything ridiculous about it. Did he *force* you to say yes?

PENELOPE He didn't have to *force* me. I had no *choice.*

RODGER I don't understand.

PENELOPE I couldn't do otherwise.

RODGER I don't understand.

PENELOPE I *wanted* to.

RODGER You wanted to do otherwise?

PENELOPE I *wanted* to *marry Harry.*

RODGER Well there you are!

PENELOPE There you are.

RODGER And if you'd wanted to say no –

PENELOPE But I didn't *want* – to say no ... I wanted to say yes, I had no choice – but to want to say yes.

RODGER Then why blame Harry?

PENELOPE I'm not blaming Harry, why do you continually get the wrong end of the stick? I don't regret marrying him. Ours is not the kind of marriage one regrets. Far from it. Never once has Harry ever behaved in any way other than as I would have expected him to. Never once has he given me the slightest cause to feel he was dissatisfied or restless or wanted to see someone else's face at the breakfast table, just for once. Our life together has been one continuous stream of marital harmony ...

CAMILLA Tell Rodger what you were aiming at, darling.

PENELOPE Aiming what at?

CAMILLA The revolver.

PENELOPE I wasn't aiming it. I just pointed it at something.

RODGER At what?

PENELOPE At a target.

RODGER Are you in the habit of doing target practice in the evening?

PENELOPE Habit has nothing to do with it. Besides, as I said, it was an accident.

CAMILLA Because you have no mice.

PENELOPE Yes, because I have no mice. And because plaster didn't fall from the ceiling and because the telephone didn't ring and because the world didn't suddenly come to an end; really, this is like an inquisition! One would think there were nothing else in the world but why I let off this silly gun! As though the whole Universe were centred in one accidental revolver shot! Really, you're both positively *medieval.*

RODGER We don't have to stay if you don't want us to.

PENELOPE I do want you to. I want to be able to talk to friends intimate enough to understand without passing judgement.

RODGER What on?

PENELOPE Me.

CAMILLA Why should we?

PENELOPE Why indeed? Why should anyone pass judgement on anyone in this strange, haphazard, accidental life?

(Pause. A sob. Penelope is crying. Rodger flaps his arms.)

CAMILLA Penelope ...

PENELOPE Don't speak to me. I don't want to be spoken to. I want absolute silence ... I know I'm being incredibly tiresome.

RODGER Not at all –

PENELOPE Don't contradict me. I am ... I'm being incredibly tiresome and gauche ... Dragging you away from your television, as though real life is more important ... I was brought up in the old-fashioned way, you see; to think of friends as friends. But of course it's all a mockery. Life isn't to be taken seriously. It's just a cheap imitation of a television play. So undramatic ... The most incredible things happen suddenly out of the blue, as though they've been stuck in by accident, and the last act doesn't resolve a thing. Life is an affront to the intelligence, I realise that; badly written, badly acted, and apparently not directed at all ...

RODGER I think you should take a sedative and go to bed.

PENELOPE What solution does that produce to which problem?

(Pause)

CAMILLA And you hit it.

PENELOPE Hit what?

CAMILLA The target.

PENELOPE What target?

CAMILLA The one you were aiming at.

PENELOPE I wasn't aiming at it, I just pointed the gun at it.

CAMILLA But you did.

PENELOPE Hit it?

CAMILLA Yes.

PENELOPE Yes.

CAMILLA Hm.

(Pause)

PENELOPE The first things I ever noticed about Harry were his intelligence and his poise. He was never surprised. This is a logical world, he used to say; why be surprised if one thing happens rather than another? If a lift breaks down there's good reason for it. So while other men would have banged on the sides with their fists and walked up and down and pressed all the buttons, Harry simply divided his *Times* in two, and he sat on the foreign news in one corner while I sat on the home news in another, and for the next twenty minutes he explained to me Einstein's Special Theory of Relativity. Life, Harry used to say, is reason. Quarrelling, Harry used to say, is the last resort of the feeble-minded. Surprise, hope and despair, Harry used to say, are the three ugly sisters in the tale of Man's quest towards intellectual maturity . . .

CAMILLA And down it fell . . .

PENELOPE Mine has been the perfect marriage!

RODGER Down what fell?

CAMILLA The target.

PENELOPE Yes, it fell down.

CAMILLA Lay down.

RODGER The target. Lay down?

PENELOPE Yes, Rodger, the target lay down.

RODGER I don't get the drift.

CAMILLA No, dear; you don't get the drift.

PENELOPE Because there isn't any drift to get.

(Pause)

CAMILLA You are so smug, Rodger.

RODGER What?

CAMILLA You're so *smug*.

RODGER What are you talking about *now*?

CAMILLA You think nothing can ever happen to you. You think nothing can ever go wrong.

RODGER Of course it can't. I've explained. I'm impregnable.

CAMILLA You're insufferable.

RODGER I don't think you'd better have any more gin, dear . . .

CAMILLA Very well . . . I have a lover.

RODGER What the devil are you on about now?

CAMILLA I have a *lover*.

RODGER Nonsense; it's not your habit to –

CAMILLA Not my habit! You don't know anything about my habits! What do you think I think of when you're away, during the day? It's been my habit for years. What are you smiling at? Haven't you noticed the gleam in my eye when you opened the door in the evening and said hallo, dear, and kissed me on the right cheek? Did you think my suppressed yawns were boredom? No, they were satiation.

RODGER I think you're going a bit far –

CAMILLA How often have I longed for a loaded revolver as you sat smugly asking if I'd had a good day?

RODGER *Really, Camilla . . .*

CAMILLA What do you know, Rodger? What – do – you – know?

(Pause. Rodger picks up the revolver, goes over to Camilla, and puts it into her hand.)

RODGER Here you are. Hold it. Point it at me. I have the courage of my convictions. Pull back the safety catch. Pull the trigger.

(She pulls the trigger. Pause)

CAMILLA Oh dear . . .

(Pause)

I didn't have any lover . . . Is that how . . .?

PENELOPE Yes. That's how it happened to me.

Biographical Notes

James Saunders was born in London in 1925. After finishing his studies at the University of Southampton he became a teacher of English. In 1949 he started writing plays, beginning with a few short pieces. But it was not until 1963 that he produced his first full-length play, "Next Time I'll Sing to You" (the story of a hermit, who spent 36 years living in a hut in a field, cutting himself off from the outside world). This play investigates the essential loneliness of man and the general meaninglessness of his life. Similar problems are discussed in his 1964 collection "Neighbours & Other Plays", which contains "A Slight Accident". Most of these plays were written during the 1950s and are concerned with life's absurdity: "Alas, Poor Fred" examines the emptiness of marital life; "Neighbours" is a study of a confrontation between a black man and a white woman; "A Slight Accident" (first produced in 1961) is concerned with the conflict between the sense of planning one's own life and the inherent unpredictability of real-life events. It may also be seen as a study in the limitations and manipulation of language. Saunders' reputation as one of Britains's top modern dramatist was further strengthened by "A Scent of Flowers" (1964/5), "The Borage Pigeon Affair" (1969) and "Hans Kolhaas" (1972).

Annotations

28 2 **becomingly** in a graceful manner - **equivocal** [ɪ'kwɪvəkl] mysterious - 4 **a woman of means** a rich woman - 7 **barrel** the metal tube of a revolver - **to fan** to wave one's hand or some object to produce a current of air - 9 **to peer** to look closely - 10 **to stoop** to bend the body forwards and downwards - 12 **to nudge** to touch slightly - 16 **tiresome** *here:* likely to cause some trouble - 18 **to have s.th. fixed** *here:* to have s.th. repaired - 25 **bearskin rug** the skin of a bear, used as a carpet - **meticulously** [mɪ'tɪkjʊləslɪ] carefully

29 1 **to and fro** backwards and forwards - **to rehearse** to practise a play, piece of music, etc. - 3 **rotten** *here:* disagreeable, very unpleasant - 6 **to drive s.o. to suicide** ['sju:ɪsaɪd] to make s.o. kill himself - 7 **to defile** [dɪ'faɪl] to make dirty - 12 **filthy** dirty, disgusting - 23 **tincture of iodine** ['tɪŋktʃərəv 'aɪədi:n] liquid for disinfecting wounds *(Jod)* - **afresh** again - 26 **Trucial Oman** ['tru:sjəl əʊ'mɑ:n] country in Arabia - 27 **vile** [vaɪl] disgusting

30 11 **to gurgle** to make a bubbling sound - 26 **to argue** to debate

31 16 **a free agent** s.o. who can choose freely how to act - 17 **account** report

32 5 **fuss** unnecessary excitement - 13 **the usual motions** *here:* the action of preparing a drink - 17 **out of the blue** unexpectedly - 18 **ludicrous occurrence** ['lu:dɪkrəs ə'kʌrəns] ridiculous event - 19 **to busy o.s.** to make or keep o.s. busy - 20 **inexplicable** impossible to explain - 29 **for camouflage** ['kæməflɑ:ʒ] in order to deceive the observer by giving a false appearance to things - 35 **to rely upon s.o.** to trust s.o. - 37 **delicacy** ['delɪkəsɪ] tact and sensitivity

33 1 **to pry into s.th.** to inquire too curiously into other people's affairs - 7 **allusion** indirect reference, hint - 17 **worked out** calculated in detail - **I daresay** I suppose - 21 **slipper** a light shoe worn in the house - 25 **to leap to conclusions** to form a judgement too quickly - 27 **woe betide you if** may misfortune come to you if - 28 **check your descent** keep you from falling down - 29 **unique** [ju:'ni:k] the only one of its kind

34 5 **one of those days** one of those days that are full of trouble - 7 **the evenings are drawing in** it is becoming dark earlier - 13 **cotton wool** *(Watte)* - 22 **stockbroker** *(Börsenmakler)* - 33 **lounge** [laʊndʒ] sitting-room - 34 **to upset** to overturn, to overthrow

35 7 **inquisitive** [ɪn'kwɪzətɪv] eager to learn details about other people's affairs - 8 **to poke around** *(coll.)* to search around - **Axminster carpet** type of carpet, called after its place of origin - 11 **to call for s.th.** to come and fetch s.th. - 14 **pole** a stick - 17 **measure** action taken *(Maßnahme)*

36 2 **to persecute s.o.** [ˈpɜːsɪkjuːt] to trouble s.o. continually – 4 **to insinuate s.th.** [ɪnˈsɪnjʊeɪt] to suggest s.th. indirectly and unpleasantly – 29 **to pursue a subject** [pəˈsjuː] to go on talking about a subject

37 6 **to pester s.o.** to annoy s.o. continually – 7 **all and sundry** everybody – 15 **imagination** power of the mind to imagine s.th. – 16 **to catalogue** [ˈkætəlɒg] to put in a list – 17 **at set intervals** regularly, at fixed times – 19 **a manual of running instructions** *here:* a handbook on how to run one's daily life – 23 **facade** [fəˈsɑːd] the front of a building, *also:* false appearance – **to lurk** to lie in wait and ready to attack – 28 **to stab** to wound or kill with a pointed instrument – 31 **to strike off** to go off – **infinite** [ˈɪnfɪnɪt] endless, unlimited – 34 **Tatler, Country Life** *(names of two magazines)* – 38 **invulnerable** that cannot be wounded or hurt – **impregnable** that resists all attacks

38 4 **to run s.o. over** to pass over s.o. in a vehicle – 5 **as safe as houses** very safe – 9 **scar** mark remaining on skin as the result of a wound – 10 **stain** dirty mark – 12 **to meet the untoward** [ˌʌntəˈwɔːd] to meet s.th. unfavourable or inconvenient – 13 **to size s.th. up** to form a judgement or opinion of s.th. – **gingerly** [ˈdʒɪndʒəlɪ] with great care and caution to avoid harming oneself – 16 **lump** a solid mass of material – 17 **hair-trigger** small tongue of metal which fires a gun or revolver at the slightest pressure – 28 **safety catch** a device which prevents a gun from being fired by accident

39 34 **deliberately** after thinking about it, on purpose – 37 **obtuse** [əbˈtjuːs] slow in understanding – **design** *here:* purpose

40 3 **I don't get the drift** I don't get the meaning – 7 **deliberation** careful consideration – **to take a sip** to drink just a few drops – 20 **mischance** [ˌmɪsˈtʃɑːns] bad luck – 34 **wainscot** wooden panelling on the lower half of the walls

41 1 **to scuttle by** to run quickly and anxiously – 9 **porter** doorman – 10 **a stray cat** a cat without a home – 12 **to fend for o.s.** to look after o.s. – 20 **to bound** to jump – 25 **by the same token** as a result of the same evidence – 36 **to prod** to push with a stick-like object – 37 **a pair of tweezers** a small tool for picking up or pulling out very small things, e.g. hairs from the eyebrows

42 1 **taxidermist** [ˈtæksɪdɜːmɪst] a person who prepares and stuffs the skin of animals so that they look as if alive – 10 **immutable** [ɪˈmjuːtəbl] unchangeable – 19 **oilskin** cloth treated with oil to make it waterproof – 31 **perforce** inevitably – 33 **a foregone conclusion** an inevitable result – 35 **gypsy** [ˈdʒɪpsɪ] a member of a wandering race, moving about in caravans and living in camps *(Zigeuner)* – 36 **to scrape** to rub s.th. along some other instrument to produce a noise – **plaintively** sounding sad – **chartreuse** [ʃɑːˈtrɜːz] *(alcoholic drink)*

43 18 **to get the wrong end of the stick** to misunderstand – 22 **dissatisfied** not content – 24 **marital** having to do with marriage – 30 **target** an aim in shooting practice, *also:* an object of attack – 35 **plaster** white material used to cover walls and ceilings - 37 **inquisition** [ˌɪnkwɪˈzɪʃn] a thorough interrogation - 40 **positively** definitely - **medieval** [ˌmedɪˈiːvl] belonging to the Middle Ages

44 2 **intimate** [ˈɪntɪmɪt] very close (e.g. a friend) - 3 **to pass judgement on s.o.** to condemn s.o. - 8 **haphazard** [hæpˈhæzəd] happening by mere chance - 9 **to flap one's arms** to move one's arms up and down or from side to side - 15 **gauche** [gəʊʃ] tactless - **to drag away** to pull away - 17 **mockery** a subject of laughter *(Hohn und Spott)* - 20 **to stick in** to put in - **to resolve** to bring about a result - 21 **affront** [əˈfrʌnt] deliberate show of disrespect, offence - 22 **to direct** to produce a play on the stage - 23 **sedative** [ˈsedətɪv] medicine which calms the nerves

45 2 **poise** balance, self-confidence - 5 **to bang on s.th.** to beat s.th. with one's fists - 7 **foreign news/home news** *(two main parts of British daily newspapers)* - 10 **the feeble-minded** persons of inferior intelligence - **despair** [dɪˈspeə] state of having lost all hope - 11 **quest** attempt to find s.th. - 12 **maturity** [məˈtjʊərɪtɪ] state of full development - 25 **smug** self-satisfied, too pleased with o.s. - 32 **insufferable** unbearable - 35 **what are you on about?** what are you talking about?

46 1 **gleam** beam of soft light - 3 **suppressed yawns** attempts to prevent one's mouth from opening when tired or bored - 4 **satiation** [ˌseɪʃɪˈeɪʃn] state of being oversatisfied - 13 **conviction** firm belief

Interpretation

First Unit: Action and Content (Part I)

(Note: For this unit the text should only have been read or listened to on the cassette available up to p.34, l.20. The appearance of Rodger provides a natural caesura between the first and the second parts of the play. A comparatively more intensive discussion of the first part is justified by the importance of the opening scenes, where the reader is gradually "tuned in" to the dramatic events of the play.)

1. What is the first event in the play and is there anything strange about it?
The initial event of the play is a revolver shot, which is heard while the curtain is still down. As the rising curtain reveals the figure of Penelope standing with a revolver still smoking in her hand and the body of Harry lying on the floor, it would seem reasonable for the play to be a tragic one. Penelope's reaction, both in words and gestures, however, is surprising in

its casualness. The expression "Oh dear ..." is normally used about annoying matters of little importance.
What other expressions does Penelope use in order to describe what she has done? She tells the body on the floor not to be "ridiculous" and calls the shooting a "joke". When she speaks to Camilla on the telephone, she tells her that she has done "something rather tiresome", which is another example of gross understatement. These reactions of hers leave us uncertain as to *why* she has shot her husband. We are interested in the *motive* for her action.

2. *How are we to imagine the setting of the play, i.e. the time, the place and the relationship between the different characters?*
a) The time seems to be evening since people are watching television.
b) The place is Harry's and Penelope's flat. Penelope asks Camilla if she could come up for a few minutes, which suggests that Camilla lives on a lower floor in the same house (this also becomes clear in the second part of the play, when Rodger talks about the different parties who live in their house, p.41, ll.7–9). It is important that Camilla does not live far away, because Penelope expects her to have heard the shot (cf. p.33, ll.13–17).
c) Harry and Penelope are husband and wife. Camilla seems to be a good friend of Penelope's.
d) The social background of the characters is upper middle class. This becomes particularly obvious from their affected speech (cf. the recording on cassette) as well as in their actions. The fact that they live in a house with several flats and a porter (p.41, ll.7–9) suggests a fashionable, upper-middle-class residential area of London.

3. *How is the TV play integrated into the play's action?* At first sight, the scene on TV may be felt to interrupt the action of the play. What goes on in the TV play seems illogical, absurd and meaningless. But there are some links between the play as a whole and the scene on TV, which should not be overlooked.
Firstly, the scene presented by the two actors and two actresses is a natural part of the play because it is that part of the television programme which Camilla watches after she comes up to Penelope's flat. She was watching it when Penelope phoned her, and Penelope suggests that she might watch the rest of it in her flat. Later it serves to explain why Camilla did not realize that the shot which she heard was fired in her neighbourhood. There must, however, be more to it than this, as the author finds it necessary to present it as a sort of "play within the play" (cf. Glossary). The term "play within the play" is justifiable, although the audience can only perceive the acoustic dimensions of the scene.

Secondly, then, it provides a foil for the events that go on in Penelope's flat. In the TV play as on the stage there are four characters (including Rodger, who shows up later), two men and two women; here as there we hear revolver shots. While we are interested in Penelope's reasons for shooting her husband and hope to discover them in the course of our play, here we know that we shall never be told why the two shots are fired, because we only witness a small extract from a TV play, where the reasons have probably already been given. Thus, there are both parallels and differences between the TV and the stage play, which have to be taken into account for the further discussion of the play (cf. Sixth unit, section 5).

4. What does Penelope do before Camilla opens the conversation? She switches the TV set on because Camilla had only consented to come up on the condition that she could go on watching. She tries to imagine how Camilla will enter the flat and actually rehearses this situation in order to be prepared ("Penelope darling ...", p.28, l.24). She covers her husband's body with a bearskin rug and arranges cushions on it in order to hide it. While Camilla is watching the TV play, she walks to and fro "rehearsing her lines", i.e. working out what she is going to tell Camilla. All these actions can be seen as Penelope's attempts to control herself, her reactions, and the situation she finds herself in.

5. Penelope has told Camilla on the phone that she has done "something rather tiresome". What reasons does she give for asking Camilla up to her flat? Twice in the play Penelope indicates her reasons for calling Camilla: While she is still on the phone, she admits her need for company. Later, when Camilla has discovered the body under the bearskin rug, she accuses her of prying and reproaches her by saying "I thought I could rely upon you as a friend" and "I took you for a woman of delicacy and understanding" (p.32, ll.34–37). She seems to expect real understanding and perhaps help from Camilla.

6. How does Penelope react when Camilla starts inquiring about Harry? First she pretends not to know about whom Camilla is talking, then she pretends not to understand Camilla's question. Finally, she turns on her, wanting to know why Camilla asked the question in the first place. When Camilla cannot give any reasons (because her question is only too natural after what Penelope has told her on the telephone), Penelope cannot stop herself from pronouncing her fears of discovery: "do you think I've murdered him or something ..." (p.31, ll.8f). So it is she herself who suggests the idea of murder to Camilla. The shallowness and ambiguity of her explanation ("As a matter of fact he is lying down." p.31, ll.9f) provokes further questions from Camilla – she inquires about Harry's state of health. Again Penelope's answer seems to be anything but well-prepared: "No. Yes. I don't know." (p.31, l.12). This pattern of innocent question and unintentionally informative answer develops into the main structural device of the play. Thus oddly enough, it is Penelope who, while giving a whole series of evasive answers, gradually lets out more and more of the true story. Both Camilla and the audience can thus slowly gather information, though we, the audience, of course, know more, because we have witnessed the beginning of the play.

7. *What does Camilla do when she discovers the camouflage? Does she understand what has happened?* Just like Penelope at the beginning of the play she stays remarkably calm. Apparently she is not shocked at all by the thought of a body covered by a bearskin rug and cushions arranged for camouflage. When Penelope ends her speech with an impassioned appeal to their friendship, Camilla carefully hints at a special kind of bond between the two women: "You're not unique, you know." (p.33, l.29). Her remark before Penelope's speech – "it could be anyone's husband" (p.33, l.12) – also becomes significant in this context. She indicates that she has had similar experiences with her husband and finally the two women seem to reach a tentative mutual understanding. We cannot, however, at this stage be sure whether Camilla can really guess the full extent of what has happened.

Homework

1. Try to give a summary of the events before and during the first part of the play as you imagine them from what is given in the dialogue and in the stage directions up to page 34.
2. The play has something of a detective story about it. Its suspense derives mainly from speculation about the motive for the criminal action. Try to imagine why Penelope shot her husband and give possible reasons. Should this not be possible, try to explain why.
3. Are there any elements in the TV play that seem comic to you?

Second Unit: Action and Content (Part II)

1. *How can the second part of the play be subdivided into shorter but still coherent passages?* The various topics brought up and the characters chiefly engaged in conversation (configuration) make further subdivisions possible:

- Rodger and Camilla on "cocoa" and upsetting the "routine" (p. 34, l.23–p.35, l.3)
- Rodger, (Camilla), and Penelope on Harry's whereabouts (p.35, l.4–p.37, l.7)
- Rodger on the advantages of a "catalogued" life (p.37, l.8–p.38, l.13)
- Rodger, Camilla and Penelope on the revolver and the relation between accident and purpose (p.38, l.14–p.41, l.39)
- Penelope on her first encounter with Harry (p.42, l.1–p.45, l.23)
- Camilla and Rodger on their marital life and their "version" of the opening scene (p.45, l.25–end).

2. Why does Rodger come up to Penelope's flat? According to what he says he comes up to remind Camilla that it is time to have her cup of cocoa, which he was just making when Camilla went to see Penelope. However, it is not only the cocoa that matters, but, as he says himself, "… it's the principle of the thing" (p.35, l.2). The routine of his everyday life, which he has "catalogued" down to its most minute detail, has been upset by Camilla leaving their flat at an unusual time.

3. How does Peneolope explain the body under the bearskin rug to him? She tells him it is a carpet wrapped in a bearskin rug, lying there with the cushions in order to be collected by the cleaners in the morning. The two shoes that are sticking out are explained by two poles which, she says, are put down the centre of the carpet to make it easier to carry and whose ends have to be covered with the shoes so that the person carrying the carpet will not be injured.

4. What information does Penelope give about Harry?
a) present situation: She says he had to go to Hull to see a client, and that he rang her from a hotel bedroom to say that he felt unwell.
b) past events: Penelope relates, that she met Harry in a lift, where they got stuck twice. This improbable event caused them to marry, because it seemed to have a special meaning: "I wanted to say yes, I had no choice – but to want to say yes." (p.43, ll.15f).
c) attitude towards life: Penelope describes Harry as an absolute rationalist who believed in the logic of the world and consequently could never be surprised by anything.

5. What story does Rodger tell to illustrate the usefulness of routine? He tells a story which he found in the newspaper that day: A hairdresser's assistant, who was quietly working along a row of seven ladies sitting under the hairdriers, suddenly grabbed a pair of scissors and stabbed all seven of them one after the other. For Rodger the reason for this mad action is absolutely clear: "he lost his respect for routine" (p.37, ll.29f). Every step away from well-ordered routine, he says, leads one into the dangers of the unknown.

6. How does Penelope "explain" her deed to Rodger and Camilla, who do not really know what she is talking about? She says it was an accident: she was just holding the revolver and "nothing happended to stop me" (p.40, ll.20f). She claims that life is haphazard and accidental and that eventually nothing can be rationally or logically explained. So her arguments do not "explain" what she has done, they only express her view of life. In this way, her own speech illustrates the meaning of her words.

7. At what point of the play does Camilla finally understand what has happened? This question cannot be satisfactorily answered by putting forth one solution alone.
a) One could argue that she already has some understanding at the end of the first part of the play, and that she only asks further questions to confirm her suspicions.
b) The view that Camilla does not understand until she herself starts attacking Rodger (p.45, l.25) seems more plausible.
c) But there are hints that she senses what has happened before that: her insistence on asking whether Penelope has hit the target seems to indicate a special purpose. Her final "Hm" (p.44, l.36) signifies a certain thoughtful expression. When she speaks again, she does so to continue a sentence which Penelope has not finished. A few lines later she makes it clear that she knows more than Rodger when she tells him: "No, dear; you don't get the drift." (p.45, l.22).

Homework
1. Give a summary of the play's action. Penelope has shot her husband Harry and calls her friend Camilla to come and keep her company. She hides Harry's body, but only partially, and answers any questions concerning him in a rather evasive manner. Camilla is followed by her husband Rodger, who complains that the routine of his everyday life has been upset by Camilla's untimely departure from their flat. Rodger discovers the camouflaged body and the revolver which Penelope used. Whereas he still asks for explanations, Camilla seems to have understood. She tells Rodger that she has a lover and that she has often wished to kill Rodger when he came home in the afternoon, upon which Rodger hands her the revolver and tells her to shoot him, not believing that she could really do anything

like that. Camilla shoots him and Penelope then admits that the same thing happened to her.

2. The ending of the play is reminiscent of its beginning. What are the similarities and differences between the two actions?

a) similarities:
- a woman shoots her husband
- reaction is casual (expression "Oh dear . . ." repeated)
- the same revolver is used and the action happens in the same flat.

b) differences:
- Penelope was not (recognizably) influenced by any previous action; Camilla shoots her husband partly because of what has gone on in the play.
- Therefore Penelope's action in the end remains without a proper "motive". (It might be argued, of course, that the fundamental contrast and mutual exclusiveness of the husbands' and the wives' views of life serve as a motive for both shootings.)
- The question of the motive for Penelope's action is not "answered" in the play, but Camilla's action serves to illustrate how it happened.

Third Unit: The Characters

1. How is Penelope, the protagonist of the play, presented? In his introductory *stage directions* the author gives us a short sketch of her outward appearance, when he writes "looking perhaps rather as might a woman of means who had just broken her husband's favourite piece of antique china" (p.28, ll.4f). From this we get the impression that she is an educated, upper middle-class, married woman. After shooting her husband, she reacts to the situation as she might have done upon breaking something valuable that belonged to her husband but was of comparatively little use to herself.
Apart from these few remarks by the author, Penelope is presented through her own *words* and *actions*. She compares killing Harry to breaking off the handle of a cup. For her, life is a random series of accidents, and in her terminology "accident" includes the fact that nothing happened to stop her from shooting her husband. When she talks about her marriage, she maintains that one has no freedom of choice in one's life; one is enslaved by "a chain of events on its immutable course" (p.42, ll.9f). Her own conclusion is that "life isn't to be taken seriously" (p.44, ll.17f), and this attitude is illustrated to the audience by the action of the whole play.

2. How does Penelope describe her husband? She only gives a description of his attitude towards life: Harry believed in "a logical world" (p.45, l.2); to him every single event was reasonable. He actually used to express this with the formula: "Life is reason" (p.45, l.9). Therefore people should never quarrel, never be surprised, never hope and never despair, i.e. get rid of all their emotions. His view of life, as can be easily seen, is in direct opposition to Penelope's.

3. What relationship can we suppose existed between Harry and Penelope? Taking their opposite views of life into account, one should expect a continuous battle or else a total misunderstanding between the two. Penelope, however, speaks of their marriage as a "continuous stream of marital harmony" (p.43, l.24). She says they never quarrelled and Harry never gave her the slightest cause to feel he was dissatisfied or restless. Ironically, this marriage has now ended by one partner shooting the other. Whereas their married life was determined by Harry's rationalist view of life, its end is brought about by Penelope's outlook. The essential contradiction between them could only be solved by the elimination of one partner.
Penelope's criticism of Harry becomes evident in the speeches in which she talks about their marital bliss (p.33, ll.18–23; p.43, ll.19–24; p.45, ll.1–12). The very qualities that she seems to be praising – Harry's refusal to quarrel, his methodicalness (bringing flowers every Thursday), his contentedness, his poise – are what finally makes her pull the trigger. In every instance Camilla understands what Penelope is really trying to express, as becomes obvious in her answers.

4. How are Camilla and Rodger presented in the play? They are both presented through their actions and words; Rodger is also characterised by a stage direction and through Camilla's words, when she compares him to Harry.
Our first impression of Camilla is that of an ardent TV viewer. Not only does she ask Penelope on the phone whether they have had their TV set repaired, but she also sits down in front of it to watch the rest of the TV play in Penelope's flat before she starts talking. She seems to be in a position similar to Penelope's as becomes evident in the conversation in which they are engaged when the door bell rings and Rodger comes in.
Rodger seems to be rather similar to Harry in that he also has a rationalist view of life, although he represents a different extreme. He has planned every minute of his everyday life, or, as he says, he believes in routine. He calls himself "a creature of habit" (p.38, ll.4f) and is convinced that

"nothing can go wrong tomorrow" because "nothing went wrong today" (p.38, ll.11f). One could call this attitude the "traditionalist" view of life. Whereas Rodger seems to think that he is "as safe as houses" (p.38, l.5) behind "the bastion of habit" (p.37, l.23), Penelope's view of him is different. "How do you know", she asks him, "what's behind the wainscot?" (p.40, ll.33f), suggesting that the "bastion" Rodger is hidden behind is no more than a "façade" as he himself had previously admitted in a slip of the tongue (p.37, l.23)

Blackboard

Though we cannot be sure about Camilla's position in the beginning, we recognize that the constellation of the characters is that of a double conflict:

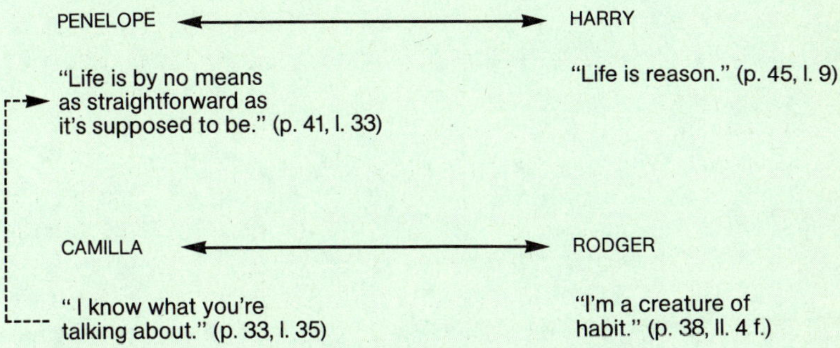

In both cases it is husband and wife who are in opposition. Whereas the two men are extremely outspoken concerning their views of life – the rationalist and the traditionalist view – the women seem to come to their own conclusions only in the course of the play and as a result of their unexpected actions. They are taken by surprise, as it seems, and their alternative view of life, which Penelope takes pains to formulate in the play, could be called the "accidentalist" attitude. In the course of the play Camilla is slowly won over to Penelope's side. Towards the end she gives up her questioning and signals her understanding (e.g. p.43, l.34).

5. The play presents a conflict between different attitudes towards life. Why do you think the author combined this conflict with the contrast between the sexes – woman vs. man? The two men in the play have to work, to organize and plan their lives, whereas the two women stay at home and spend their days with housework and TV – a pattern which corresponds to a widespread cliché. Beside the traditional view of role differentiation, James Saunders seems to be upholding another cliché: that men tend to be logical, whereas women tend to be irrational. He then uses this cliché to support the point he is making: that the representatives of logic/reason and tradition are bound to fail in the face of the absurdity of everyday life. The real life of the characters is not affected: e.g. we should not ask what will become of Penelope and Camilla after they have shot their husbands. As characters in a play they are meant to illustrate a more general conflict, they come to stand for a set of attitudes. The fact that the two women kill their husbands should not be interpreted as an act of feminist assertion against the rule of men. What Saunders wants to say in this play is that no system of categories or convictions, be it rationalist or traditionalist, can survive the unexpectedness of real-life events.

6. The four characters of the play represent fundamentally different attitudes towards life. In this respect they differ from real-life persons. Try to describe the difference between a real-life person and a dramatic character. The dramatic character is a construction of the playwright's imagination: he is defined by the author's description, the dialogue and the action. Our impression of real-life persons is not limited in this way: though it, too, is determined by their action and environment, we can still imagine that different situations will reveal new facets of the same character, who is therefore never wholly determined.
The dramatic character is thus an abstraction. In *A Slight Accident*, moreover, all the characters may be said to be "flat", i.e. they are determined by one dominant trait and do not develop in the course of the play. (It may be argued, of course, that Camilla, in being brought over to Penelope's side, does in fact experience a change of attitude.)
Since the information we are given about a stage character cannot but be limited, every detail becomes much more important than with real-life persons. In drama even the smallest detail is intentional and therefore relevant, whereas in life we have continually to assess which bit of information we consider relevant and which accidental or irrelevant. In this play, for example, we are not told much about the past and the present situation of the characters or the motives for their actions, and yet we tend to speculate about this kind of background information. The play, however, tells us – in Penelope's words – that this is unimportant, that life is inexplicable, and death nothing "but a slight accident".

Homework
The constellation of characters.

Fourth Unit: Language

1. In the play there are two central statements about language. What are they and what attitude towards language do they express?
a) "words are important. What do we have to play with but words?" (p.31, ll.31f).
b) "Language is so limited." (p.34, l.10).
Language is not to be taken seriously. It is something "to play with". Words can be manipulated, their meaning can differ according to the purpose for which a speaker uses them. Therefore it becomes difficult to achieve real understanding by language alone. Penelope feels this to be a basic limitation which is inherent in language.

2. How does the play illustrate the problems of human communication caused by language? The problems of language are illustrated in two ways which involve manipulation and the limitation of language respectively:
a) *Indirect use of language*, i.e. metaphor, euphemism, comparison, irony. The words are used to express something beyond their literal meaning.
b) *Ambiguity*, i.e. words have two or more meanings, which leads to misunderstanding.
Whereas the indirect use of language is an intentional form of communication, ambiguity may be unintentional and inherent in language itself.

3. Find examples of the indirect use of language in the play.
Euphemisms and understatements: Penelope calls her killing of Harry "a joke" and "something rather tiresome", and tells Camilla that her husband "isn't much company at the moment" (p.28, ll.11, 16f). Later she tells her that Harry is "lying down" (p.31, l.10). The effect of these word plays is heightened by the fact that they are repeated (partly by other characters) during the play (e.g. p.31, l.35; p.33, ll.9f; p.35, ll.29–39).
Comparisons: "It's like breaking the handle off a cup" (p.31, ll.37f). "Suppose, for instance, there'd been a mouse." and the ensuing story of cats and mice (p.40, l.24–p.41, l.27).
Metaphor: "the normal course of events carrying itself along as usual, in a nice straight grey line" (p.32, ll.16f); "Behind the facade, no, the bastion of habit, of routine, anarchy lurks, waiting to spring" (p.37, ll.22–24); "the well-ordered terrain of habituality ... into the jungle of infinite possibility, where every step is into unknown country" (p.37, ll.30–32); "You think we stand on the banks of the river of life, all dressed up in our oilskins of habit catching events like salmon as they leap past." (p.42, ll.18f).
Irony: The metaphors used by Penelope can be seen as instances of irony, as

can all her explanations about life, which she sums up in her sentence "Life isn't to be taken seriously. It's just a cheap imitation of a television play. So undramatic ..." (p.44, ll.17–19).

4. Find examples of ambiguity in the play.
"We've had it fixed ... the picture is perfect now" (p.28, ll.18f) could also ironically refer to a previous quarrel which has now been settled.
"All the interesting characters are dead already" (p.30, l.30) could refer to the play itself and not merely to the TV play.
The discussion of the terms "by accident", "on purpose" and "deliberately" (p.31, l.37–p.32, l.2; p.39, l.15–p.40, l.21): whereas "by accident" is the antonym of both "on purpose" and "deliberately", these two expressions are not completely synonymous, as Penelope struggles to explain. This and her quibbling about the difference between "aiming at" and "pointing at" (p.43, l.28; p.44, l.31) are attemps on her part to put across her "accidentalist" view and to evade the responsibility for her action.
The pun on "Leeds" (p.36, ll.10–20).
The question "what were you aiming at" (p.43, l.25) could also refer to the purpose or aim of an action, and not only the target of a revolver.

5. When concerned with communication in a play, we must distinguish between two levels on which language becomes effective:
a) The inner system of communication, i.e. communication among the characters. So far we have mainly been concerned with this level.
b) The outer system of communication, i.e. communication between the playwright and the audience (or the readers). The language of a play works on both these levels, so we also have to look at the function of language in the communication between playwright and audience.

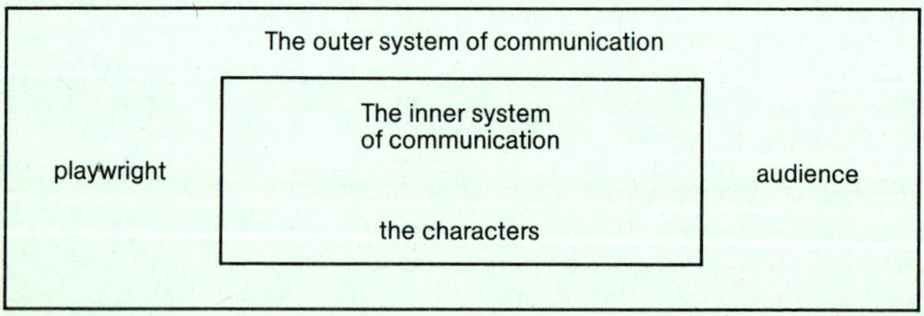

6. What is the effect on the audience of most of the devices of dramatic language we have discussed so far? The euphemisms, comparisons and ambiguities of the play have a comic effect. This results, basically, from the incongruity of the initial action of the play, which we expect to be treated as a serious or tragic event, with the way in which this action is discussed later on. The author's essential device for achieving this effect is irony. The title of the play indicates that the author wants the audience to view the play's events from an ironic point of view. On the level of author-audience communication therefore, irony is the chief dramatic device. Penelope's ironic use of metaphor is only one means of expressing this.

7. Are there other comic elements which are not part of the inner system of communication, i.e. which are only recognized as comic by the audience and not by the characters of the play?
a) Camilla's entrance which corresponds exactly to Penelope's rehearsal of the scene that the audience has witnessed just a moment before.
b) Camilla's description of the camouflaged body, which is totally correct, as the audience knows, but which is vehemently contradicted by Penelope.
c) Rodger's repeating the word "cocoa" five times and yet claiming: "It isn't the cocoa, dear, it's the principle of the thing." (p.35, l.2).
d) Penelope's desperate explanations of the body under the bearskin rug and of Harry's present situation.
e) Penelope's evasive manner whenever she is asked about what has happened, connected with her repeatedly pouring drinks.
f) Camilla's remark "it could be anybody's husband" (p.33, l.12) is an example of dramatic irony (cf. Glossary) as it anticipates, as it were, her own killing of Roger.
g) Penelope's preposterous explanation of why she considers her action an accident (p.40, l.20–p.41, l.27).
h) the short descriptions of Penelope and Rodger in the stage directions are, of course, not part of the inner system of communication. To the author they offer a further means of expressing the overall irony of the play.

8. The play also comments on set expressions used in everyday communication. Give examples. After Penelope's statement that she has not broken the handle off a cup, Camilla replies by saying, "I see". Penelope explodes the emptiness of this small-talk formula by challenging Camilla: "You don't see." (p.32, ll.8f). A little later Camilla asks Penelope, "You won't think I'm prying?", expecting a negative answer such as "Of course not". Penelope's honest reply "Probably" (p.33, ll.39f) again breaks the even flow of a small-talk conversation. (See also p.35, ll.3–6.)
The ample use of clichés of polite conversation (e.g. "I do like your curtains ...", p.32, l.14); "The evenings are drawing in ...", p.34, l.7), which are quite meaningless in the context, is characteristic of the middle-class idiom

and at the same time demonstrates that the characters are trying to hide behind a veil of language. Understatement and polite formulas are part of their composure or, to use Rodger's words, part of the facade behind which anarchy lurks. The reliance on set formulas goes so far that the linguistic behaviour of the characters becomes predictable, as Penelope demonstrates when she anticipates Camilla's words at the beginning of the play.

9. How is the limitation of language demonstrated to the audience? The linguistic means at the characters' disposal as well as the type of social intercourse typical of their class proves inadequate for dealing with the extraordinary. It might do for broken cup handles, but not for violent death. Thus the limitation of language finds its expression in the fact that the answer to the question why Penelope killed her husband is not expressed in words but merely suggested by Camilla's final action. As Penelope puts it, "nearly everything we do is – inexplicable" (p.32, l.20).

Blackboard

	"What do we have to play with but words?" (p.31, ll.31f) ↓ MANIPULATION of language	"Language is so limited." (p.34, l.10) ↓ LIMITATION of language
inner system of communication	indirect use of language (euphemism, comparison, metaphor)	ambiguity
outer system of communication	irony	meaning not expressed by words but by action

Homework

1. Why can the play to some extent be called a play about language?
2. *A Slight Accident* can be seen as one of a great number of modern plays which are concerned with the problems of language. Why do you think has language become a problem in the 20th century?
3. Are there any similarities between *A Slight Accident* and *A Separate Peace* in so far as the treatment of language is concerned?

Fifth Unit: Structure and Themes

1. What do you think is the theme / are the themes of the play?

a) a wife shooting her husband for no clear-cut reason
b) different and opposing attitudes towards life
c) the failure of language as a means of communication.

(Note: These or similar answers should be collected and remain on the blackboard until the end of the discussion.)

(a) refers to the *action* of the play, (b) expresses the *underlying conflict* of the play, and (c) refers to the *dialogue*. Which of the three we consider as the central theme of the play largely depends on our personal judgement – not only as to what this particular play is about but also as to which element we consider the most essential to drama – action, ideas, or language.

2. When we look at the action of the play, we see that it starts with Penelope shooting her husband. How is the ensuing quest for the motive for this action structured?

a) by the subsequent appearance of two new characters and
b) by the gradual discoveries and recognitions of these two "detectives".

It is interesting to trace the different motions which Penelope goes through between the urges to confess and to conceal what has happened:

Blackboard:

Part I presents the initial event and reveals Penelope's indecision. It ends with a half-hearted confession to Camilla.

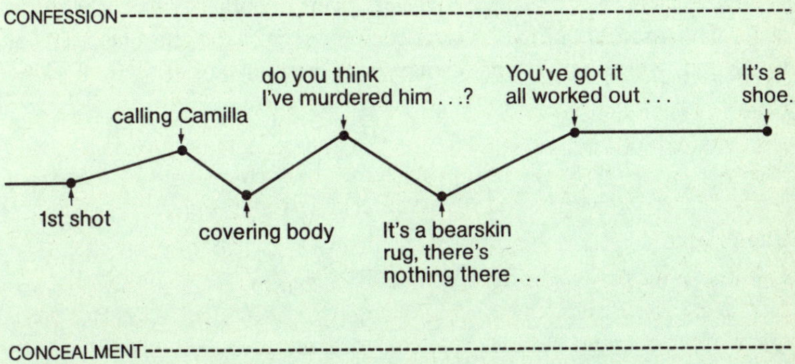

Part II begins with a new attempt to conceal what has happened. It lasts until the revolver is discovered. After that there is a gradual move towards confession.

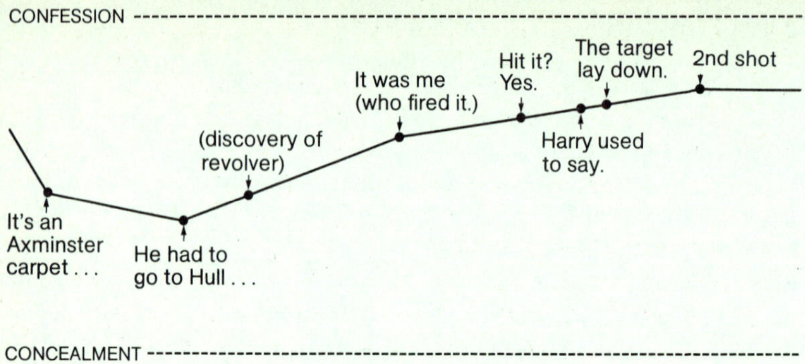

The reason why Penelope does not confess immediately despite her obvious wish to do so – witness the imperfect camouflage and the many clues she gives – is that she feels that language can only inadequately convey how the "accident" happened. Whereas Camilla and Rodger might perhaps be called "detectives", Penelope, the "criminal", is only too eager to let the truth come out, but in *her* way. She finally does so by bringing about a situation which is more or less identical with the one preceding the opening of the play and which leads to Camilla killing Rodger.

3. Draw a diagram depicting the suspense in the play. Even though the play's level of suspense is very high from the first shot to the last, we feel a new rise in suspense with every turn of events. It is followed each time by a gradual decline, when Penelope tries to divert the others from their suspicions. The discovery of the revolver could be seen as the "turning point" of the action, which has its final climax in the second shot at the end of the play.

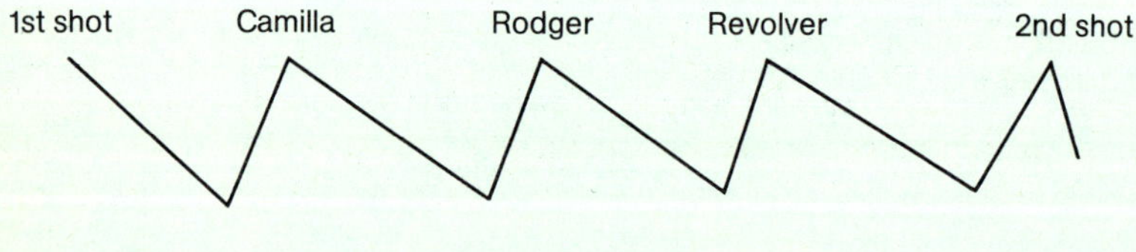

4. *We have seen that the underlying conflict in the play is between different attitudes towards life. Describe them and give examples from the play.*

RATIONALIST VIEW (Harry)	TRADITIONALIST VIEW (Rodger)
– life is logical; every single event is meaningful	– life is dangerous, a realm of infinite possibilities
– therefore there is no need for fear, anger, hope and despair	– therefore man should plan his life: only habit and routine can give safety.
↓	↓

"I have the courage of my convictions." (p.46, ll.12f)

↓

↑

The beginning and the end of the play illustrate the superiority of the

ACCIDENTALIST VIEW OF LIFE (Penelope & Camilla)

- life is haphazard, an inexplicable, immutable chain of events
- therefore explanations are futile, planning is useless: "events [are] catching us" (p.42, l.20).

The importance of this theme for the work of James Saunders is underlined in a statement the author himself made: "If there is any theme that runs through all of my work, it's the absurdity of finding logic in anything at all." (Quoted in Dieter A. Berger, "James Saunders: *The Borage Pigeon Affair*", in: Horst Oppel, ed., *Das englische Drama der Gegenwart*, Berlin 1976, p.174).

5. *Does the form of the play support its central idea, i.e. the superiority of the accidentalist view of life?* We have already seen that both shots, i.e. the beginning and the end of the play, support the accidentalist view. In between, however, the play's structure is rather reminiscent of a detective story, which is based upon the rationalist assumption that every action has an underlying motive and that this motive can be discovered by deduction. But this is not exactly what happens in the play. There is no one person who could really be called a detective. Neither Camilla nor Rodger knows about the initial action when they enter Penelope's flat, and consequently they cannot intentionally wish to find a reason for it. All that goes on between the two shots is a random collection of questions and answers and explanations with none of the characters following a plan. If in the end the audience

can guess what the motive of Penelope's action was, this is entirely due to their singular position of knowing more than the characters and therefore being able to understand more of Penelope's answers than the other characters in the play can. The form of the play, the structure of its action, can therefore be said to support what the play is trying to convey.

Homework

1. Describe the structure of the play's action.
2. At what point in the play does Penelope finally lose control and become compelled to reveal more and more of what has happened?

Sixth Unit: The Dramatic Text and the Play on the Stage (optional)

1. Do you think it is more difficult for the reader to follow the text of a play than that of a novel or a short story?
While reading a play we have to perform a double task:
a) Whe have to read the words and understand their meaning and
b) We have to imagine how the stage directions and the dialogue could be translated into stage pictures and theatrical action.
The latter task requires a much greater effort than imagining the characters, the situation and the action of a novel, because the narrator usually provides all the information and comment necessary. A playwright, however, cannot give too many details, because his play is meant to be performed, i.e. directed and acted in a theatre. Every performance of a play will be different according to the conditions of the particular stage, the directors and the actors. Knowing of these influences upon his play, a playwright tends to restrict himself to only the most necessary information.

2. What details are we given about the setting of A Slight Accident? There is no change of scene in the play. The setting is Harry's and Penelope's flat (unity of place). The information we are given about it is that it contains a telephone, a TV set, a bearskin rug and several cushions, that it is situated on the third floor of a house, and that there must be a cocktail-cabinet, where Penelope can pour out drinks.

3. What is the time structure of the play? The time structure of the play consists of a linear progression without any interruption (unity of time). This means that the time we spend reading or seeing the play, corresponds to the time which is presented in the play.

4. The words are brought to life by the actors who speak them. What elements in the play provide a kind of prestructuring of the dialogue?

a) The text is interspersed with pauses of different length:

- three dots indicate a short pause after which the subject is pursued by the same character; the preceding word or words are emphasized.
- stage directions like "slight pause" or "pause" either indicate a change of subject or that the speaker has to think before he starts again. In either case they tend to emphasize the following line.

b) Sometimes stress is indicated by italics, e.g. "I mean we *pretend*, Rodger, we *pretend* ..." (p.42, l.12), "So there *was* an extra shot." (p.39, l.11).

c) Some words or sentences gain special importance by being repeated in the play, e.g. "a joke", "by accident", "on purpose", "I don't get the drift", "Oh dear ..."

d) There are also a few instances of sound repetition or rhyme-like orchestration of sentences, e.g.

PENELOPE	He's out of	town.		
RODGER	Out of	town?	PENELOPE	Yes.
RODGER	I thought he was in	town,		
PENELOPE	He was in	town,		
	now he's out of	town.		
CAMILLA	Not lying	down.		
RODGER	Out of	town,		
	not lying	down?		
PENELOPE	He's out of	town		
	lying	down. (p.35)		

5. What effect does the TV play within the play have upon the audience? The two women are on the stage, one of them watching the TV play, which starts off with two women quarrelling. This incorporation of a play within the play presents the audience with their own situation, i.e. sitting and watching two women in a play. We are spectators of a play just like Camilla is a TV viewer. While we are likely to take the play as a representation of life itself, the TV play in its theatrical exaggeration is clearly recognized as the presentation of a fictional world. And yet, the similarities between the TV play and the play on the stage provide the audience with the problem of deciding what is "real" about life. The function of the play within the play is to make the audience more conscious of the fictional quality of the play on the stage.

The play within the play may have yet another function. In one of her comments Penelope compares life with a TV play: "Life isn't to be taken seriously. It's just a cheap imitation of a television play. So undramatic ... The most incredible things happen suddenly out of the blue, as though they've been stuck in by accident, and the last act doesn't resolve a thing. Life is an affront to the intelligence, I realise that; badly written, badly acted, and apparently not directed at all ..." (p.44, ll.17–22). If life is only a bad imitation of a TV play and if the TV play we have witnessed at the beginning is taken to be representative, then Penelope is making a strong point indeed. (Note: Penelope's words seem to echo the famous lines from Macbeth's monologue:

> Life's but a walking shadow; a poor player,
> That struts and frets his hour upon the stage,
> And then is heard no more: it is a tale
> Told by an idiot, full of sound and fury,
> Signifying nothing. (*Macbeth*, Act V, Scene 5, ll.24–28)

If the class has already read *Macbeth* it might be asked to comment on this parallel.)

Homework

1. Discuss Penelope's comparison of life with a TV play in the light of your own everyday experience.
2. Does watching TV influence people's way of looking at life?

Harold Pinter

A Slight Ache

A country house, with two chairs and a table laid for breakfast at the centre of the stage. These will later be removed and the action will be focused on the scullery on the right and the study on the left, both indicated with a minimum of scenery and props. A large well kept garden is suggested at the back of the stage with flower beds, trimmed hedges, etc. The garden gate, which cannot be seen by the audience, is off right.
Flora and Edward are discovered sitting at the breakfast table. Edward is reading the paper.

FLORA Have you noticed the honeysuckle this morning?
EDWARD The what?
FLORA The honeysuckle.
EDWARD Honeysuckle? Where?
FLORA By the back gate, Edward.
EDWARD Is that honeysuckle? I thought it was ... convolvulus, or something.
FLORA But you know it's honeysuckle.
EDWARD I tell you I thought it was convolvulus.
(Pause)
FLORA It's in wonderful flower.
EDWARD I must look.
FLORA The whole garden's in flower this morning. The clematis. The convolvulus. Everything. I was out at seven. I stood by the pool.
EDWARD Did you say – that the convolvulus was in flower?
FLORA Yes.
EDWARD But good God, you just denied there was any.
FLORA I was talking about the honeysuckle.
EDWARD About the what?
FLORA *(calmly)* Edward – you know that shrub outside the toolshed ...
EDWARD Yes, yes.
FLORA That's convolvulus.
EDWARD That?
FLORA Yes.
EDWARD Oh. *(Pause)* I thought it was japonica.

FLORA Oh, good Lord no.

EDWARD Pass the teapot, please.

(Pause. She pours tea for him.)

I don't see why I should be expected to distinguish between these plants. It's not my job.

FLORA You know perfectly well what grows in your garden.

EDWARD Quite the contrary. It is clear that I don't.

(Pause)

FLORA *(rising)* I was up at seven. I stood by the pool. The peace. And everything in flower. The sun was up. You should work in the garden this morning. We could put up the canopy.

EDWARD The canopy? What for?

FLORA To shade you from the sun.

EDWARD Is there a breeze?

FLORA A light one.

EDWARD It's very treacherous weather, you know.

(Pause)

FLORA Do you know what today is?

EDWARD Saturday.

FLORA It's the longest day of the year.

EDWARD Really?

FLORA It's the height of summer today.

EDWARD Cover the marmalade.

FLORA What?

EDWARD Cover the pot. There's a wasp. *(He puts the paper down on the table.)* Don't move. Keep still. What are you doing?

FLORA Covering the pot.

EDWARD Don't move. Leave it. Keep still.

(Pause)

Give me the "Telegraph".

FLORA Don't hit it. It'll bite.

EDWARD Bite? What do you mean, bite? Keep still. *(Pause)* It's landing.

FLORA It's going in the pot.

EDWARD Give me the lid.

FLORA It's in.

EDWARD Give me the lid.

FLORA I'll do it.

EDWARD Give it to me! Now . . . Slowly . . .

FLORA What are you doing?

EDWARD Be quiet. Slowly . . . carefully . . . on . . . the . . . pot! Ha-ha-ha. Very good.

(He sits on a chair to the right of the table.)

FLORA Now he's in the marmalade.

EDWARD Precisely.

(Pause. She sits on a chair to the left of the table and reads the "Telegraph".)

FLORA Can you hear him?

EDWARD Hear him?

FLORA Buzzing.

EDWARD Nonsense. How can you hear him? It's an earthenware lid.

FLORA He's becoming frantic.

EDWARD Rubbish. Take it away from the table.

FLORA What shall I do with it?

EDWARD Put it in the sink and drown it.

FLORA It'll fly out and bite me.

EDWARD It will not bite you! Wasps don't bite. Anyway, it won't fly out. It's stuck. It'll drown where it is, in the marmalade.

FLORA What a horrible death.

EDWARD On the contrary.

(Pause)

FLORA Have you got something in your eyes?

EDWARD No. Why do you ask?

FLORA You keep clenching them, blinking them.

EDWARD I have a slight ache in them.

FLORA Oh dear.

EDWARD Yes, a slight ache. As if I hadn't slept.

FLORA Did you sleep, Edward?

EDWARD Of course I slept. Uninterrupted. As always.

FLORA And yet you feel tired.

EDWARD I didn't say I felt tired. I merely said I had a slight ache in my eyes.

FLORA Why is that, then?

EDWARD I really don't know.

(Pause)

FLORA Oh goodness!

EDWARD What is it?

FLORA I can see it. It's trying to come out.

EDWARD How can it?

FLORA Through the hole. It's trying to crawl out, through the spoon-hole.

EDWARD Mmmnn, yes. Can't do it, of course. *(Silent pause.)* Well, let's kill it, for goodness' sake.

FLORA Yes, let's. But how?

EDWARD Bring it out on the spoon and squash it on a plate.

FLORA It'll fly away. It'll bite.

EDWARD If you don't stop saying that word I shall leave this table.

FLORA But wasps do bite.

EDWARD They don't bite. They sting. It's snakes . . . that bite.

FLORA What about horseflies?

(Pause)

EDWARD *(to himself)* Horseflies suck.

(Pause)

FLORA *(tentatively)* If we . . . if we wait long enough, I suppose it'll choke to death. It'll suffocate in the marmalade.

EDWARD *(briskly)* You do know I've got work to do this morning, don't you? I can't spend the whole day worrying about a wasp.

FLORA Well, kill it.

EDWARD You want to kill it?

FLORA Yes.

EDWARD Very well. Pass me the hot water jug.

FLORA What are you going to do?

EDWARD Scald it. Give it to me. *(She hands him the jug. Pause.)* Now . . .

FLORA *(whispering)* Do you want me to lift the lid?

EDWARD No, no, no. I'll pour down the spoon hole. Right . . . down the spoon-hole.

FLORA Listen!

EDWARD What?

FLORA It's buzzing.

EDWARD Vicious creatures. *(Pause)* Curious, but I don't remember seeing any wasps at all, all summer, until now. I'm sure I don't know why. I mean, there must have been wasps.

FLORA Please.

EDWARD This couldn't be the first wasp, could it?

FLORA Please.

EDWARD The first wasp of summer? No. It's not possible.

FLORA Edward.

EDWARD Mmmmnnn?

FLORA Kill it.

EDWARD Ah, yes. Tilt the pot. Tilt. Aah . . . down here . . . right down . . . blinding him . . . that's . . . it.

FLORA Is it?

EDWARD Lift the lid. All right, I will. There he is! Dead. What a monster. *(He squashes it on a plate.)*

FLORA What an awful experience.

EDWARD What a beautiful day it is. Beautiful. I think I shall work in the garden this morning. Where's that canopy?

FLORA It's in the shed.

EDWARD Yes, we must get it out. My goodness, just look at that sky. Not a cloud. Did you say it was the longest day of the year today?

FLORA Yes.

EDWARD Ah, it's a good day. I feel it in my bones. In my muscles. I think I'll stretch my legs in a minute. Down to the pool. My God, look at that flowering shrub over there. Clematis. What a wonderful ... *(He stops suddenly.)*

FLORA What? *(Pause)* Edward, what is it? *(Pause)* Edward ...

EDWARD *(thickly)* He's there.

FLORA Who?

EDWARD *(low, murmuring)* Blast and damn it, he's there, he's there at the back gate.

FLORA Let me see. *(She moves over to him to look. Pause. Lightly)* Oh, it's the matchseller.

EDWARD He's back again.

FLORA But he's always there.

EDWARD Why? What is he doing there?

FLORA But he's never disturbed you, has he? The man's been standing there for weeks. You've never mentioned it.

EDWARD What is he doing there?

FLORA He's selling matches, of course.

EDWARD It's ridiculous. What's the time?

FLORA Half past nine.

EDWARD What in God's name is he doing with a tray full of matches at half past nine in the morning?

FLORA He arrives at seven o'clock.

EDWARD Seven o'clock?

FLORA He's always there at seven.

EDWARD Yes, but you've never ... actually seen him arrive?

FLORA No, I ...

EDWARD Well, how do you know he's ... not been standing there all night? *(Pause)*

FLORA Do you find him interesting, Edward?

EDWARD *(casually)* Interesting? No. No, I . . . don't find him interesting.

FLORA He's a very nice old man, really.

EDWARD You've spoken to him?

FLORA No. No, I haven't spoken to him. I've nodded.

EDWARD *(pacing up and down)* For two months he's been standing on that spot, do you realise that? Two months. I haven't been able to step outside the back gate.

FORA Why on earth not?

EDWARD *(to himself)* It used to give me great pleasure, such pleasure, to stroll along through the long grass, out through the back gate, pass into the lane. That pleasure is now denied me. It's my own house, isn't it? It's my own gate.

FLORA I really can't understand this, Edward.

EDWARD Damn. And do you know I've never seen him sell one box? Not a box. It's hardly surprising. He's on the wrong road. It's not a road at all. What is it? It's a lane, leading to the monastery. Off everybody's route. Even the monks take a short cut to the village, when they want to go . . . to the village. No one goes up it. Why doesn't he stand on the main road if he wants to sell matches, by the *front* gate? The whole thing's preposterous.

FLORA *(going over him)* I don't know why you're getting so excited about it. He's a quiet, harmless old man, going about his business. He's quite harmless.

EDWARD I didn't say he wasn't harmless. Of course he's harmless. How could he be other than harmless?

(Fade out and silence)

(Flora's voice, far in the house, drawing nearer)

FLORA *(off)* Edward, where are you? Edward? Where are you, Edward? *(She appears.)* Edward? Edward, what are you doing in the scullery?

EDWARD *(looking through the scullery window)* Doing?

FLORA I've been looking everywhere for you. I put up the canopy ages ago. I came back and you were nowhere to be seen. Have you been out?

EDWARD No.

FLORA Where have you been?

EDWARD Here.

FLORA I looked in your study. I even went into the attic.

EDWARD *(tonelessly)* What would I be doing in the attic?

FLORA I couldn't imagine what had happened to you. Do you know it's twelve o'clock?

EDWARD Is it?

FLORA I even went to the bottom of the garden, to see if you were in the toolshed.

EDWARD *(tonelessly)* What would I be doing in the toolshed?

FLORA You must have seen me in the garden. You can see through this window.

EDWARD Only part of the garden.

FLORA Yes.

EDWARD Only a corner of the garden. A very small corner.

FLORA What are you doing here?

EDWARD Nothing. I was digging out some notes, that's all.

FLORA Notes?

EDWARD For my essay.

FLORA Which essay?

EDWARD My essay on space and time.

FLORA But ... I've never ... I don't know that one.

EDWARD You don't know it?

FLORA I thought you were writing one about the Belgian Congo.

EDWARD I've been engaged on the dimensionality and continuity of space ... and time ... for years.

FLORA And the Belgian Congo?

EDWARD *(shortly)* Never mind about the Belgian Congo.

(Pause)

FLORA But you don't keep notes in the scullery.

EDWARD You'd be surprised. You'd be highly surprised.

FLORA Good Lord, what's that? Is that a bullock let loose? No. It's the matchseller! My goodness, you can see him ... through the hedge. He looks bigger. Have you been watching him? He looks ... like a bullock. *(Pause)* Edward? *(Pause. Moving over to him)* Are you coming outside? I've put up the canopy. You'll miss the best of the day. You can have an hour before lunch.

EDWARD I've no work to do this morning.

FLORA What about your essay? You don't intend to stay in the scullery all day, do you?

EDWARD Get out. Leave me alone.

(A slight pause)

FLORA Really Edward. You've never spoken to me like that in all your life.

EDWARD Yes, I have.

FLORA Oh, Weddie. Beddie-Weddie . . .

EDWARD Do not call me that!

FLORA Your eyes are bloodshot.

EDWARD Damn it.

FLORA It's too dark in here to peer . . .

EDWARD Damn.

FLORA It's so bright outside.

EDWARD Damn.

FLORA And it's dark in here.

(Pause)

EDWARD Christ blast it!

FLORA You're frightened of him.

EDWARD I'm not.

FLORA You're frightened of a poor old man. Why?

EDWARD I am not!

FLORA He's a poor, harmless old man.

EDWARD Aaah my eyes.

FLORA Let me bathe them.

EDWARD Keep away. *(Pause. Slowly)* I want to speak to that man. I want to have a word with him. *(Pause)*

It's quite absurd, of course. I really can't tolerate something so . . . absurd, right on my doorstep. I shall not tolerate it. He's sold nothing all morning. No one passed. Yes. A monk passed. A non-smoker. In a loose garment. It's quite obvious he was a non-smoker but still, the man made no effort. He made no effort to clinch a sale, to rid himself of one of his cursed boxes. His one chance, all morning, and he made no effort.

(Pause)

I haven't wasted my time. I've hit, in fact, upon the truth. He's not a matchseller at all. The bastard isn't a matchseller at all. Curious I never realised that before. He's an impostor. I watched him very closely. He made no move towards the monk. As for the monk, the monk made no move towards him. The monk was moving along the lane. He didn't pause, or halt, or in any way alter his step. As for the matchseller – how ridiculous to go on calling him by that title. What a farce. No, there is something very false about that man. I intend to get to the bottom of it. I'll soon get rid of him. He can go and ply his trade somewhere else. Instead of standing like a bullock . . . a bullock, outside my back gate.

FLORA But if he isn't a matchseller, what is his trade?

EDWARD We'll soon find out.

FLORA You're going out to speak to him?

EDWARD Certainly not! Go out to *him*? Certainly ... not. I'll invite him in here. Into my study. Then we'll ... get to the bottom of it.

FLORA Why don't you call the police and have him removed?

(He laughs. Pause)

Why don't you call the police, Edward? You could say he was a public nuisance. Although I ... I can't say I find him a nuisance.

EDWARD Call him in.

FLORA Me?

EDWARD Go out and call him in.

FLORA Are you serious? *(Pause)* Edward, I could call the police. Or even the vicar.

EDWARD Go and get him.

(She goes out. Silence. Edward waits.)

FLORA *(in the garden)* Good morning.

(Pause)

We haven't met. I live in this house here. My husband and I.

(Pause)

I wonder if you could ... would you care for a cup of tea?

(Pause)

Or a glass of lemon? It must be so dry, standing here.

(Pause)

Would you like to come inside for a little while? It's much cooler. There's something we'd very much like to ... tell you, that will benefit you. Could you spare a few moments? We won't keep you long.

(Pause)

Might I buy your tray of matches, do you think? We've run out, completely, and we always keep a very large stock. It happens that way, doesn't it? Well, we can discuss it inside. Do come. This way. Ah now, do come. Our house is full of curios, you know. My husband's been rather a collector. We have goose for lunch. Do you care for goose? *(She moves to the gate.)* Come and have lunch with us. This way. That's ... right. May I take your arm? There's a good deal of *nettle* inside the gate. *(The matchseller appears.)* Here. This way. Mind now. Isn't it beautiful weather? It's the longest day of the year today.

(Pause)

That's honeysuckle. And that's convolvulus. There's clematis. And do you see that plant by the conservatory? That's japonica.

(Silence. She enters the study.)

FLORA He's here.

EDWARD I know.

FLORA He's in the hall.

EDWARD I know he's here. I can smell him.

FLORA Smell him?

EDWARD I smelt him when he came under my window. Can't you smell the house now?

FLORA What are you going to do with him, Edward? You won't be rough with him in any way? He's very old. I'm not sure if he can hear, or even see. And he's wearing the oldest –

EDWARD I don't want to know what he's wearing.

FLORA But you'll see for yourself in a minute, if you speak to him.

EDWARD I shall.

(Slight pause)

FLORA He's an old man. You won't . . . be rough with him?

EDWARD If he's so old, why doesn't he seek shelter . . . from the storm?

FLORA But there's no storm. It's summer, the longest day . . .

EDWARD There was a storm, last week. A summer storm. He stood without moving, while it raged about him.

FLORA When was this?

EDWARD He remained quite still, while it thundered all about him.

(Pause)

FLORA Edward . . . are you sure it's wise to bother about all this?

EDWARD Tell him to come in.

FLORA I . . .

EDWARD Now.

(She goes and collects the matchseller.)

FLORA Hullo. Would you like to go in? I won't be long. Up these stairs here. *(Pause)* You can have some sherry before lunch. *(Pause)* Shall I take your tray? No. Very well, take it with you. Just . . . up those stairs. The door at the . . . *(She watches him move.)* the door . . . *(Pause)* the door at the top. I'll join you . . . later.

(She goes out.)

(The matchseller stands on the threshold of the study.)

EDWARD *(cheerfully)* Here I am. Where are you?

(Pause)

Don't stand out there, old chap. Come into my study. *(He rises.)* Come in.

(The matchseller enters.)

That's right. Mind how you go. That's ... it. Now, make yourself comfortable. Thought you might like some refreshment, on a day like this. Sit down, old man. What will you have? Sherry? Or what about a double scotch? Eh?
(Pause)
I entertain the villagers annually, as a matter of fact. I'm not the squire, but they look upon me with some regard. Don't believe we've got a squire here any more, actually. Don't know what became of him. Nice old man he was. Great chess-player, as I remember. Three daughters. The pride of the county. Flaming red hair. Alice was the eldest. Sit yourself down, old chap. Eunice I think was number two. The youngest one was the best of the bunch. Sally. No, no, wait a minute, no, it wasn't Sally, it was ... Fanny. Fanny. A flower. You must be a stranger here. Unless you lived here once, went on a long voyage and have lately returned. Do you know the district?
(Pause)
Now, now, you mustn't ... stand about like that. Take a seat. Which one would you prefer? We have a great variety, as you see. Can't stand uniformity. Like different seats, different backs. Often when I'm working, you know, I draw up one chair, scribble a few lines, put it by, draw up another, sit back, ponder, put it by ... *(absently)* ... sit back ... put it by ...
(Pause)
I write theological and philosophical essays ...
(Pause)
Now and again I jot down a few observations on certain tropical phenomena – not from the same standpoint, of course. *(Silent pause)* Yes. Africa, now. Africa's always been my happy hunting ground. Fascinating country. Do you know it? I get the impression that you've ... been around a bit. Do you by any chance know the Membunza Mountains? Great range south of Katambaloo. French Equatorial Africa, if my memory serves me right. Most extraordinary diversity of flora and fauna. Especially fauna. I understand in the Gobi Desert you can come across some very strange sights. Never been there myself. Studied the maps though. Fascinating things, maps.
(Pause)
Do you live in the village? I don't often go down, of course. Or are you passing through? On your way to another part of the country? Well, I can tell you, in my opinion you won't find many prettier parts than here. We

win the first prize regularly, you know, the best kept village in the area. Sit down.

(Pause)

I say, can you hear me?

(Pause)

I said, I say, can you hear me?

(Pause)

You possess most extraordinary repose, for a man of your age, don't you? Well, perhaps that's not quite the right word ... repose. Do you find it chilly in here? I'm sure it's chillier in here than out. I haven't been out yet, today, though I shall probably spend the whole afternoon working, in the garden, under my canopy, at my table, by the pool.

(Pause)

Oh, I understand you met my *wife*? Charming woman, don't you think? Plenty of grit there, too. Stood by me through thick and thin, that woman. In season and out of season. Fine figure of a woman she was, too, in her youth. Wonderful carriage, flaming red hair. *(He stops abruptly.)*

(Pause)

Yes, I ... I was in much the same position myself then as you are now, you understand. Struggling to make my way in the world. I was in commerce too. *(With a chuckle)* Oh, yes, I know what it's like – the weather, the rain, beaten from pillar to post, up hill and down dale ... the rewards were few ... winters in hovels ... up till all hours working at your thesis ... yes, I've done it all. Let me advise you. Get a good woman to stick by you. Never mind what the world says. Keep at it. Keep your shoulder to the wheel. It'll pay dividends.

(Pause)

(With a laugh.) You must excuse my chatting away like this. We have few visitors this time of the year. All our friends summer abroad. I'm a home bird myself. Wouldn't mind taking a trip to Asia Minor, mind you, or to certain lower regions of the Congo, but Europe? Out of the question. Much too noisy. I'm sure you agree. Now look, what will you have to drink? A glass of ale? Curaçao Fockink Orange? Ginger beer? Tia Maria? A Wachenheimer Fuchsmantel Riesling Beerenauslese? Gin and it? Chateauneuf-du-Pape? A little Asti Spumante? Or what do you say to a straightforward Piesporter Goldtröpfchen Feine Auslese (Reichsgraf von Kesselstaff)? Any preference?

(Pause)

You look a trifle warm. Why don't you take off your balaclava? I'd find that a little itchy myself. But then I've always been one for freedom of

movement. Even in the depth of winter I wear next to nothing.
(Pause)
I say, can I ask you a personal question? I don't want to seem inquisitive but aren't you rather on the wrong road for matchselling? Not terribly busy, is it? Of course you may not care for petrol fumes or the noise of traffic. I can quite understand that.
(Pause)
Do forgive me peering but is that a glass eye you're wearing?
(Pause)
Do take off your balaclava, there's a good chap, put your tray down and take your ease, as they say in this part of the world. *(He moves towards him.)* I must say you keep quite a good stock, don't you? Tell me, between ourselves, are those boxes full, or are there just a few half-empty ones among them? Oh yes, I used to be in commerce. Well now, before the good lady sounds the gong for petit déjeuner will you join me in an apéritif? I recommend a glass of cider. Now ... just a minute ... I know I've got some – Look out! Mind your tray!

(The tray falls, and the matchboxes.)

Good God, what ...?
(Pause)
You've dropped your tray.

(Pause. He picks the matchboxes up.)

(Grunts) Eh, these boxes are all wet. You've no right to sell wet matches, you know. Uuuuugggh. This feels suspiciously like fungus. You won't get very far in this trade if you don't take care of your goods. *(Grunts, rising.)* Well, here you are.
(Pause)
Here's your tray.

(He puts the tray into the matchseller's hands, and sits. Pause)

Now listen, let me be quite frank with you, shall I? I really cannot understand why you don't sit down. There are four chairs at your disposal. Not to mention the hassock. I can't possibly talk to you unless you're settled. Then and only then can I speak to you. Do you follow me? You're not being terribly helpful. *(Slight pause.)* You're sweating. The sweat's pouring out of you. Take off that balaclava.
(Pause)

Go into the corner then. Into the corner. Go on. Get into the shade of the corner. Back. Backward.

(Pause)

Get back!

(Pause)

Ah, you understand me. Forgive me for saying so, but I had decided that you had the comprehension of a bullock. I was mistaken. You understand me perfectly well. That's right. A little more. A little to the right. Aaah. Now you're there. In shade, in shadow. Good-o. Now I can get down to brass tacks. Can't I?

(Pause)

No doubt you're wondering why I invited you into this house? You may think I was alarmed by the look of you. You would be quite mistaken. I was not alarmed by the look of you. I did not find you at all alarming. No, no. Nothing outside this room has ever alarmed me. You disgusted me, quite forcibly, if you want to know the truth.

(Pause)

Why did you disgust me to that extent? That seems to be a pertinent question. You're no more disgusting than Fanny, the squire's daughter, after all. In appearance you differ but not in essence. There's the same ...

(Pause)

The same ...

(Pause)

(In a low voice) I want to ask you a question. Why do you stand outside my back gate, from dawn till dusk, why do you pretend to sell matches, why ...? What is it, damn you. You're shivering. You're sagging. Come here, come here ... mind your tray! *(Edward rises and moves behind a chair.)* Come, quick quick. There. Sit here. Sit ... sit in this.

(The matchseller stumbles and sits. Pause)

Aaaah! You're sat. At last. What a relief. You must be tired. *(Slight pause)* Chair comfortable? I bought it in a sale. I bought all the furniture in this house in a sale. The same sale. When I was a young man. You too, perhaps. You too, perhaps.

(Pause)

At the same time, perhaps!

(Pause)

(Muttering) I must get some air. I must get a breath of air. *(He goes to the door.)* Flora!

FLORA Yes?

EDWARD *(with great weariness)* Take me into the garden.

(Silence. They move from the study door to a chair under a canopy.)

FLORA Come under the canopy.

EDWARD Ah. *(He sits.)*

(Pause)

The peace. The peace out here.

FLORA Look at our trees.

EDWARD Yes.

FLORA Our own trees. Can you hear the birds?

EDWARD No, I can't hear them.

FLORA But they're singing, high up, and flapping.

EDWARD Good. Let them flap.

FLORA Shall I bring your lunch out here? You can have it in peace, and a quiet drink, under your canopy.

(Pause)

How are you getting on with your old man?

EDWARD What do you mean?

FLORA What's happening? How are you getting on with him?

EDWARD Very well. We get on remarkably well. He's a little ... reticent. Somewhat withdrawn. It's understandable. I should be the same, perhaps, in his place. Though, of course, I could not possibly find myself in his place.

FLORA Have you found out anything about him?

EDWARD A little. A little. He's had various trades, that's certain. His place of residence is unsure. He's ... he's not a drinking man. As yet, I haven't discovered the reason for his arrival here. I shall in due course ... by nightfall.

FLORA Is it necessary?

EDWARD Necessary?

FLORA *(quickly sitting on the right arm of the chair)* I could show him out now, it wouldn't matter. You've seen him, he's harmless, unfortunate ... old, that's all. Edward – listen – he's not here through any ... design, or anything, I know it. I mean, he might just as well stand outside our back gate as anywhere else. He'll move on. I can ... make him. I promise you. There's no point in upsetting yourself like this. He's an old man, weak in the head ... that's all.

(Pause)

EDWARD You're deluded.

FLORA Edward –

EDWARD *(rising)* You're deluded. and stop calling me Edward.

FLORA You're not still frightened of him?

EDWARD Frightened of him? Of *him*? Have you *seen* him?

(Pause)

He's like jelly. A great bullockfat of jelly. He can't see straight. I think as a matter of fact he wears a glass eye. He's almost stone deaf ... almost ... not quite. He's very nearly dead on his feet. Why should he frighten me? No, you're a woman, you know nothing. *(Slight pause.)* But he possesses other faculties. Cunning. The man's an impostor and he knows I know it.

FLORA I'll tell you what. Look. Let me speak to him. I'll speak to him.

EDWARD *(quietly)* And I know he knows I know it.

FLORA I'll find out all about him, Edward. I promise you I will.

EDWARD And he knows I know.

FLORA Edward! Listen to me! I can find out all about him, I promise you. I shall go and have a word with him now. I shall ... get to the bottom of it.

EDWARD You? It's laughable.

FLORA You'll see – he won't bargain for me. I'll surprise him. He'll ... he'll admit everything.

EDWARD *(softly)* He'll admit everything, will he?

FLORA You wait and see, you just –

EDWARD *(hissing)* What are you plotting?

FLORA I know exactly what I shall –

EDWARD What are you plotting? *(He seizes her arms.)*

FLORA Edward, you're hurting me!

(Pause)

(With dignity) I shall wave from the window when I'm ready. Then you can come up. I shall get to the truth of it, I assure you. You're much too heavy-handed, in every way. You should trust your wife more, Edward. You should trust her judgement, and have a greater insight into her capabilities. A woman ... a woman will often succeed, you know, where a man must invariably fail.

(Silence. She goes into the study.)

Do you mind if I come in?

(The door closes.)

Are you comfortable? *(Pause)* Oh, the sun's shining directly on you. Wouldn't you rather sit in the shade? *(She sits down.)*
It's the longest day of the year today, did you know that? Actually the year has flown. I can remember Christmas and that dreadful frost. And the floods! I hope you weren't here in the floods. We were out of danger up

here, of course, but in the valleys whole families I remember drifted away on the current. The country was a lake. Everything stopped. We lived on our own preserves, drank elderberry wine, studied other cultures.

(Pause)

Do you know, I've got a feeling I've seen you before, somewhere. Long before the flood. You were much younger. Yes, I'm really sure of it. Between ourselves, were you ever a poacher? I had an encounter with a poacher once. It was a ghastly rape, the brute. High up on a hillside cattle track. Early spring. I was out riding on my pony. And there on the verge a man lay – ostensibly injured, lying on his front, I remember, possibly the victim of a murderous assault, how was I to know? I dismounted, I went to him, he rose, I fell, my pony took off, down to the valley. I saw the sky through the trees, blue. Up to my ears in mud. It was a desperate battle.

(Pause)

I lost.

(Pause)

Of course, life was perilous in those days. It was my first canter unchaperoned.

(Pause)

Years later, when I was a Justice of the Peace for the county, I had him in front of the bench. He was there for poaching. That's how I know he was a poacher. The evidence though was sparse, inadmissible, I acquitted him, letting him off with a caution. He'd grown a red beard, I remember. Yes. A bit of a stinker.

(Pause)

I say, you are perspiring, aren't you? Shall I mop your brow? With my chiffon? Is it the heat? Or the closeness? Or confined space? Or . . .? *(She goes over to him.)* Actually, the day is cooling. It'll soon be dusk. Perhaps it is dusk. May I? You don't mind?

(Pause. She mops his brow.)

Ah, there, that's better. And your cheeks. It is a woman's job, isn't it? And I'm the only woman on hand. There.

(Pause. She leans on the arm of chair.)

(Intimately) Tell me, have you a woman? Do you like women? Do you ever . . . think about women?

(Pause) Have you ever . . . stopped a woman? *(Pause)*

I'm sure you must have been quite attractive once. *(She sits.)* Not any more, of course. You've got a vile smell. Vile. Quite repellent, in fact.

(Pause)

Sex, I suppose, means nothing to you. Does it ever occur to you that sex is a very vital experience for other people? Really, I think you'd amuse me if you weren't so hideous. You're probably quite amusing in your own way. *(Seductively)* Tell me all about love. Speak to me of love.

(Pause)

God knows what you're saying at this very moment. It's quite disgusting. Do you know when I was a girl I loved ... I loved ... I simply adored ... what *have* you got on, for goodness sake? A jersey? It's clogged. Have you been rolling in mud? *(Slight pause)* You haven't been rolling in mud, have you? *(She rises and goes over to him.)* And what have you got under your jersey? Let's see. *(Slight pause)* I'm not tickling you, am I? No. Good ... Lord, is this a vest? That's quite original. Quite original. *(She sits on the arm of his chair.)* Hmmnn, you're a solid old boy, I must say. Not at all like a jelly. All you need is a bath. A lovely lathery bath. And a good scrub. A lovely lathery scrub. *(Pause)* Don't you? It will be a pleasure. *(She throws her arms round him.)* I'm going to keep you. I'm going to keep you, you dreadful chap, and call you Barnabas. Isn't it dark, Barnabas? Your eyes, your eyes, your great big eyes.

(Pause)

My husband would never have guessed your name. Never. *(She kneels at his feet. Whispering)* It's me you were waiting for, wasn't it? You've been standing waiting for me. You've seen me in the woods, picking daisies, in my apron, my pretty daisy apron, and you came and stood, poor creature, at my gate, till death us do part. Poor Barnabas. I'm going to put you to bed. I'm going to put you to bed and watch over you. But first you must have a good whacking great bath. And I'll buy you pretty little things that will suit you. And little toys to play with. On your deathbed. Why shouldn't you die happy?

(A shout from the hall)

EDWARD Well? *(Footsteps upstage.)* Well?

FLORA Don't come in.

EDWARD Well?

FLORA He's dying.

EDWARD Dying? He's not dying.

FLORA I tell you, he's very ill.

EDWARD He's not dying! Nowhere near. He'll see you cremated.

FLORA The man is desperately ill!

EDWARD Ill? You lying slut. Get back to your trough!

FLORA Edward . . .

EDWARD *(violently)* To your trough!

(She goes out. Pause)

(Coolly) Good evening to you. Why are you sitting in the gloom? Oh, you've begun to disrobe. Too warm? Let's open these windows, then, what? *(He opens the windows.)* Pull the blinds. *(He pulls the blinds.)* And close . . . the curtains . . . again. *(He closes the curtains.)* Ah. Air will enter through the side chinks. Of the blinds. And filter through the curtains. I hope. Don't want to suffocate, do we?

(Pause)

More comfortable? Yes. You look different in darkness. Take off all your togs, if you like. Make yourself at home. Strip to your buff. Do as you would in your own house.

(Pause)

Did you say something?

(Pause)

Did you say something?

(Pause)

Anything? Well then, tell me about your boyhood. Mmnn?

(Pause)

What did you do with it? Run? Swim? Kick the ball? You kicked the ball? What position? Left back? Goalie? First reserve?

(Pause)

I used to play myself. Country house matches, mostly. Kept wicket and batted number seven.

(Pause)

Kept wicket and batted number seven. Man called – Cavendish, I think had something of your style. Bowled left arm over the wicket, always kept his cap on, quite a dab hand at solo whist, preferred a good round of prop and cop to anything else.

(Pause)

On wet days when the field was swamped.

(Pause)

Perhaps you don't play cricket.

(Pause)

Perhaps you never met Cavendish and never played cricket. You look less and less like a cricketer the more I see of you. Where did you live in those days? God damn it, I'm entitled to know something about you! You're in my blasted house, on my territory, drinking my wine, eating my duck! Now you've had your fill you sit like a hump, a mouldering heap. In my room. My den. I can rem ... *(He stops abruptly.)*

(Pause)

You find that funny? Are you grinning?

(Pause)

(In disgust) Good Christ, is that a grin on your face? *(Further disgust)* It's lopsided. It's all – down on one side. You're grinning. It amuses you, does it? When I tell you how well I remember this room, how well I remember this den. *(Muttering)* Ha. Yesterday now, it was clear, clearly defined, so clearly.

(Pause)

The garden, too, was sharp, lucid, in the rain, in the sun.

(Pause)

My den, too, was sharp, arranged for my purpose ... quite satisfactory.

(Pause)

The house too, was polished, all the banisters were polished, and the stair rods, and the curtain rods.

(Pause)

My desk was polished, and my cabinet.

(Pause)

I was polished. *(Nostalgic)* I could stand on the hill and look through my telescope at the sea. And follow the path of the three-masted schooner, feeling fit, well aware of my sinews, their suppleness, my arms lifted holding the telescope, steady, easily, no trembling, my aim was perfect, I could pour hot water down the spoon hole, yes, easily, no difficulty, my grasp firm, my command established, my life was accounted for, I was ready for my excursions to the cliff, down the path to the back gate, through the long grass, no need to watch for the nettles, my progress was fluent, after my long struggling against all kinds of usurpers, disreputables, lists, literally lists of people anxious to do me down, and my reputation down, my command was established, all summer I would breakfast, survey my landscape, take my telescope, examine the overhanging of my hedges, pursue the narrow lane past the monastery, climb the hill, adjust the lens *(he mimes a telescope)*, watch the progress of the three-masted schooner, my progress was as sure, as fluent ...

(Pause. He drops his arms.)

Yes, yes, you're quite right, it is funny.

(Pause)

Laugh your bloody head off! Go on. Don't mind me. No need to be polite.

(Pause)

That's right.

(Pause)

You're quite right, it is funny. I'll laugh with you! *(He laughs.)* Ha-ha-ha! Yes! You're laughing with me, I'm laughing with you, we're laughing together!

(He laughs and stops.)

(Brightly.) Why did I invite you into this room? That's your next question, isn't it? Bound to be.

(Pause)

Well, why not, you might say? My oldest acquaintance. My nearest and dearest. My kith and kin. But surely correspondence would have been as satisfactory ... more satisfactory? We could have exchanged postcards, couldn't we? What? Views, couldn't we? Of sea and land, city and village, town and country, autumn and winter ... clocktowers ... museums ... citadels ... bridges ... rivers ...

(Pause)

Seeing you stand, at the back gate, such close proximity, was not at all the same thing.

(Pause)

What are you doing? You're taking off your balaclava ... you've decided not to. No, very well then, all things considered, did I then invite you into this room with express intention of asking you to take off your balaclava, in order to determine your resemblance to – some other person? The answer is no, certainly not, I did not, for when I first saw you you wore no balaclava. No headcovering of any kind, in fact. You looked quite different without a head – I mean without a hat – I mean without a headcovering, of any kind. In fact every time I have seen you you have looked quite different to the time before.

(Pause)

Even now you look different. Very different.

(Pause)

Admitted that sometimes I viewed you through dark glasses, yes, and sometimes through light glasses, and on other occasions bare eyed, and on other occasions through the bars of the scullery window, or from the roof, the roof, yes, in driving snow, or from the bottom of the drive in thick fog, or from the roof again in blinding sun, so blinding, so hot, that I had to skip and jump and bounce in order to remain in one place. Ah, that's good for a guffaw, is it? That's good for a belly laugh? Go on, then. Let it out. Let yourself go, for God's ... *(He catches his breath.)* You're crying ...

(Pause)

(Moved) You haven't been laughing. You're crying.

(Pause)

You're weeping. You're shaking with grief. For me. I can't believe it. For my plight. I've been wrong.

(Pause)

(Briskly) Come, come, stop it. Be a man. Blow your nose for goodness sake. Pull yourself together.

(He sneezes.) Ah. *(He rises. Sneeze.)* Ah. Fever. Excuse me. *(He blows his nose.)* I've caught a cold. A germ. In my eyes. It was this morning. In my eyes. My eyes.

(Pause. He falls to the floor.)

Not that I had any difficulty in seeing you, no, no, it was not so much my sight, my sight is excellent – in winter I run about with nothing on but a pair of polo shorts – no, it was not so much any deficiency in my sight as the airs between me and my object – don't weep – the change of air, the currents obtaining in the space between me and my object, the shades they make, the shapes they take, the quivering, the eternal quivering – please stop crying – nothing to do with heat-haze. Sometimes, of course, I would take shelter, shelter to compose myself. Yes, I would seek a tree, a cranny of bushes, erect my canopy and so make shelter. And rest. *(Low murmur)* And then I no longer heard the wind or saw the sun. Nothing entered, nothing left my nook. I lay on my side in my polo shorts, my fingers lightly in contact with the blades of grass, the earthflowers, the petals of the earthflowers flaking, lying on my palm, the underside of all the great foliage dark, above me, but it is only afterwards I say the foliage was dark, the petals flaking, then I said nothing, I remarked nothing, things happened upon me, then in my times of shelter, the shades, the petals, carried themselves, carried their bodies upon me, and nothing entered my nook, nothing left it.

(Pause)

But then, the time came. I saw the wind. I saw the wind, swirling, and the dust at my back gate, lifting, and the long grass, scything together ... *(Slowly, in horror)* You *are* laughing. You're laughing. Your face. Your body. *(Overwhelming nausea and horror)* Rocking ... gasping ... rocking ... shaking ... rocking ... heaving ... rocking ... You're laughing at me! Aaaaahhhh!

(The matchseller rises. Silence)

You look younger. You look extraordinarily ... youthful.

(Pause)

You want to examine the garden? It must be very bright, in the moonlight. *(Becoming weaker)* I would like to join you ... explain ... show you ... the garden ... explain ... The plants ... where I run ... my track ... in training ... I was number one sprinter at Howells ... when a stripling ... no more than a stripling ... licked ... men twice my strength ... when a stripling ... like yourself.

(Pause)

(Flatly) The pool must be glistening. In the moonlight. And the lawn. I remember it well. The cliff. The sea. The three-masted schooner.

(Pause)

(With great, final effort – a whisper) Who are you?

FLORA *(off)* Barnabas?

(Pause. She enters.)

Ah, Barnabas. Everything is ready.

(Pause)

I want to show you my garden, your garden. You must see my japonica, my convolvulus ... my honeysuckle, my clematis.

(Pause)

The summer is coming. I've put up your canopy for you. You can lunch in the garden, by the pool. I've polished the whole house for you.

(Pause)

Take my hand.

(Pause. The matchseller goes over to her.)

Yes. Oh, wait a moment.

(Pause)

Edward. Here is your tray.

(She crosses to Edward with the tray of matches, and puts it in his hands. Then she and the matchseller start to go out as the curtain falls slowly.)

Biographical Notes

Harold Pinter was born in Hackney, East London, in 1930, the only son of a Jewish tailor. After attending Hackney Downs Grammar School, Pinter received a grant and began studying at the Royal Academy of Dramatic Art. In 1949, he became a repertory actor; at this time he started writing prose and poetry. It was not until 1957 that he attempted to write drama: "The Room", his first play (which is said to have been written in two days), was followed by "The Dumb Waiter" and "The Birthday Party" in the same year. "The Caretaker" (1959) brought him critical acclaim. The 60s and 70s saw Pinter establishing a world-wide reputation through other full-length stage plays, "The Homecoming" (1965), "Old Times" (1971) and "Betrayal" (1978), and a growing number of shorter plays (for the stage, radio, and television), the most interesting of which are "A Slight Ache", "The Lover", "The Collection", "Landscape" and "Silence". Pinter has also written the scripts for several films.
Pinter's plays have often been stamped with the label "Absurd Drama", though Pinter himself would be the first to object to any attempt to look for a common denominator in his plays.
"A Slight Ache" was originally conceived as a radio play and broadcast on the BBC Third Programme on 29 July 1959. On 18 January 1961, it was presented at the Arts Theatre, London.

Annotations

50 2 **focused** ['fəʊkəst] centred – 3 **scullery** a little room near the kitchen where dishes and pans are washed – **study** a room used for studying and writing – 4 **props** (*short for:* stage properties) articles (e.g. pieces of furniture) used on stage – 9 **honeysuckle** *(Geißblatt)* – 14 **convolvulus** [kən'vɒlvjʊləs] *(Winde)* – 21 **clematis** [klɪ'meɪtɪs] *(Waldrebe)* – 28 **shrub** a low bush – **toolshed** a small building in the garden where garden tools are kept – 33 **japonica** [dʒə'pɒnɪkə] a type of ornamental bush

51 11 **canopy** ['kænəpɪ] a hanging cover fixed above a seat – 14 **breeze** a light wind – 16 **treacherous** ['tretʃərəs] deceptive and dangerous – 22 **the height of summer** [haɪt] the longest day of summer – 25 **wasp** [wɒsp] a flying insect with a sting in the tail – 30 **the 'Telegraph'** (*short for:* 'The Daily Telegraph') a British newspaper

52 10 **earthenware** ['ɜ:θnweə] made of baked clay - 11 **frantic** wildly anxious - 17 **stuck** unable to move - 23 **to clench** to close tightly - **to blink one's eyes** to shut and open them quickly

53 4 **to squash** [ɒ] to press so as to kill - 11 **to suck** to draw liquid into the mouth - 13 **tentatively** hesitantly; *here:* in an uncertain voice - 13/14 **to choke** = **to suffocate** ['sʌfəkeɪt] to die because of lack of air - 15 **briskly** quickly - 22 **to scald** [skɔ:ld] to hurt or kill by burning with hot liquid - 29 **vicious** ['vɪʃəs] cruel, dangerous - 39 **to tilt s.th.** to cause s.th. to lean to one side

54 19 **Blast and damn it** *(sl.) (a curse)*

55 11 **to stroll along** [strəʊl] to walk without haste - 12 **lane** a narrow road between fields, walls, hedges, etc. - 17 **monastery** ['mɒnəstrɪ] a building in which monks live - 18 **short cut** ['-,-] a route that is quicker than the usual one - 20 **preposterous** [prɪ'pɒstərəs] absurd, completely unreasonable - 25 **other than** anything but - 37 **attic** a room immediately below the roof

56 13 **to dig out** to find by searching - 20 **Belgian Congo** *now:* Zaire - 21 **dimensionality** [dɪ,menʃə'nælətɪ] - **continuity** [,kɒntɪ'nju:ətɪ] the state of being continuous, uninterrupted - 28 **bullock** ['bʊlək] a young bull

57 3 **bloodshot** *of eyes:* red - 5 **to peer** to look very carefully - 11 **Christ blast it!** *(a curse)* - 23 **garment** an article of clothing - 25 **to clinch a sale** *(coll.)* to sell something - **to rid o.s. of s.th.** to get rid of s.th.; *here:* to sell - **cursed** [kɜ:sɪd] damned - 30 **impostor** [ɪm'pɒstə] a person who deceives others by pretending to be s.o. or s.th. else - 33 **to alter** ['ɔ:ltə] to change - 35 **to get to the bottom of s.th.** to inquire into the cause of s.th. - 36 **to ply one's trade** to go about one's business

58 5 **public nuisance** ['nju:sns] person who behaves in such a way as to be troublesome to others - 11 **vicar** ['vɪkə] a priest in charge of a church - 23 **to benefit s.o.** to be useful to s.o. - 26 **to run out of s.th.** to have no more of s.th. - 27 **stock** supply - 29 **curio** *(short for:* curiosity*)* an object that is interesting because it is rare or unusual - 32 **nettle** wild plant *(Brennessel)* - 33 **to mind** *here:* to pay attention, to be careful - 37 **conservatory** [kən'sɜ:vətrɪ] glass house

59 16 **shelter** protection - 19 **to rage** *of storms:* to be very violent - 34 **threshold** [θreʃhəʊld] plank under a doorway, entrance - 37 **chap** *(coll.)* fellow, old friend

60 7 **to entertain** *here:* to provide food and drink at a party - **squire** the main landowner in a village - 8 **regard** *here:* respect - 12 **Eunice** ['ju:nɪs] - 13 **bunch** *(coll.)* group - 20 **to scribble** to write very quickly - **to put s.th. by** to put s.th. aside - 26 **to jot s.th. down** to write s.th. down hurriedly - 27 **phenomena** *(pl.)* [fə'nɒmɪnə] (*sg.* phenomenon) - 33 **to understand** *here:* to have been informed

61 8 **repose** [rɪ'pəʊz] quiet manner that doesn't betray any feelings - 10 **chilly** cold - 15 **grit** great courage; determination - 16 **in season and out of season** at any

time – 17 **carriage** [ˈkærɪdʒ] *here:* the way a person stands and walks – 21 **chuckle** a quiet laugh – 22 **from pillar to post** from one place to another – **up hill and down dale** *(poet.)* up the hills and down to the valley – 23 **hovel** [ˈhɒvl] miserable place to live in – **thesis** a long article written for a university degree – 25 **to keep one's shoulder to the wheel** to make an effort, to go on working – 26 **to pay dividends** to produce a benefit, an advantage – 28 **to chat away** to talk continuously without a clear purpose – 29 **to summer** *(rare)* to spend the summer – 30 **Asia Minor** [ˈeɪʒəˈmaɪnə] *(Kleinasien)* – **mind you** believe me – 34 **gin and it** gin and vermouth – 39 **a trifle warm** rather warm – **balaclava** [ˌbæləˈklɑːvə] a warm woollen headcovering that leaves the face free, but covers the head, ears, and neck – 40 **itchy** tickling in an annoying way

62 1 **next to nothing** almost nothing – 3 **inquisitive** [ɪnˈkwɪzətɪv] eager to learn details about other people's affairs – 5 **petrol fumes** nasty-smelling gases coming from cars – 10 **there's a good chap** *(a phrase expressing satisfaction with someone's behaviour, esp. that of obedient children or dogs)* – 24 **fungus** [ˈfʌŋgəs] a soft whitish growth that forms on old food, etc. – 30 **frank** sincere, open – 32 **hassock** a small bench for kneeling on (in church, etc.)

63 9 **to get down to brass tacks** *(coll.)* to start talking about the really important problems – 15 **to disgust s.o.** to cause a feeling of strong dislike in s.o. – 16 **forcibly** strongly – 18 **pertinent** relevant – 20 **in essence** [ˈesns] in one's inner nature – 25 **from dawn till dusk** from daybreak to nightfall – 26 **damn you** *(sl.) (a strong way of expressing surprise, anger, etc.)* – **to shiver** to tremble from cold or fear – **to sag** to sink down slowly – 30 **you're sat** you are seated – 31 **sale** *here:* auction

64 1 **with great weariness** [ˈwɪərɪnɪs] expressing extreme tiredness – 11 **to flap** to move (the wings) up and down – 19 **reticent** [ˈretɪsənt] shy and silent – 20 **withdrawn** habitually quiet, not concerned with what other people say – 25 **in due course** at the appropriate time – 29 **to show s.o. out** to accompany s.o. to the door – 31 **design** *here:* evil purpose, intention, plan – 37 **deluded** misled, mistaken

65 4 **jelly** a sweet soft food substance that shakes when moved; *here:* any semi-solid substance – **bullockfat** a heap of fat as big as a bullock – 6 **to be dead on one's feet** to be too exhausted to stand on one's feet – 8 **cunning** cleverness in deceiving – 16 **to bargain for s.o. or s.th.** to be prepared for s.o. or s.th. – 20 **to plot** to plan secretly – 27 **heavy-handed** nod skilful, not careful – 36 **actually** really – 37 **to fly** *here:* to pass very quickly

66 2 **current** [ˈkʌrənt] a continuously moving mass of water – 3 **preserves** food that can be kept for a long time by a special treatment *(Eingemachtes)* – **elderberry** *(Holunderbeere)* – 7 **poacher** person who hunts illegally – **encounter** a sudden or unexpected meeting – 8 **ghastly** terrible – **rape** crime of having sex with a woman against her will - **brute** a brutal person - 9 **verge** the border of a road or path - 10 **ostensibly** apparently but not really - 11 **assault** attack - **to dismount** to get down from one's horse - 17 **perilous** dangerous - **my first canter unchaperoned** [ˌʌnˈʃæpərəʊnd] my first ride without an older person to accompany and protect me - 20 **Justice of the Peace** person acting as a judge in the lowest courts - 21 **bench** *here:* the seat of a judge - 22 **sparse** *here:* scanty, not sufficient - **inadmissible** that cannot be allowed - **to acquit** to declare a person not guilty - 23 **caution** *here:* a warning given by a judge - 24 **stinker** *(sl.)* a mean or despicable person - 26 **to perspire** to sweat - **to mop** to dry by rubbing with cloth - 27 **chiffon** [ˈʃɪfɒn] scarf made of thin material - **closeness** condition of being warm and humid - **confined** limited - 38 **vile** unpleasant, nasty - **repellent** causing dislike

67 2 **vital** important - 3 **hideous** [ˈhɪdɪəs] extremely ugly, repellent - 4 **seductively** *here:* in a voice that contains an invitation to sex - 8 **jersey** a warm woollen pullover - **clogged** covered with dirt - 12 **vest** a sleeveless undergarment - 15 **lathery** [ˈlɑːðərɪ] full of foam produced by the mixture of soap and water - **scrub** the act of cleaning by hard rubbing - 23 **daisy** a small white flower *(Gänseblümchen)* - 25 **till death us do part** till death separates us (part of the pledge taken by bride and bridegroom during the marriage ceremony in church) - 27 **whacking** *(coll.)* very big - 37 **nowhere near** *here:* not at all - **to cremate s.o.** [krɪˈmeɪt] to burn s.o. at a special funeral ceremony - **He'll see you cremated.** He'll outlive you. - 39 **slut** a woman who acts immorally - **trough** [trɒf] a long narrow object for holding food or water for animals

68 4 **gloom** semi-darkness - 5 **to disrobe** to undress - 6 **blinds** cloth or other material pulled down from a roller to cover a window - 8 **chink** narrow opening in the blinds - 12 **togs** *(coll.)* clothes - **to strip to the buff** *(coll.)* to take off all clothes - 22 **goalie** *(coll.)* goalkeeper - 24 **wicket** *in cricket:* three upright sticks which the batsman tries to defend and the bowler tries to hit - **to keep wicket** to act as the player who stands behind the wicket to catch the ball - 25 **to bat** *in cricket:* to hit the ball - 28 **bowled left arm** threw the ball over his shoulder with a straight left arm - 29 **to be a dab hand at** *(coll.)* to be very clever or good at - **solo whist** a card game - **prop and cop** a special way to play solo whist - 32 **swamped** [ɒ] too wet to play on - 38 **to be entitled to** to have the right to - 39 **blasted** damned

69 1 **to have one's fill** to eat and drink as much as one can - **hump** shapeless mass - **to moulder** to decay slowly (like a corpse) - 2 **den** a room in which one works, study - 7 **lopsided** having one side heavier or lower than the other - 12 **lucid** [ˈluːsɪd] *(poet)* bright - 16 **banisters** (Geländer) - **stair rods** metal sticks used to keep the carpeting on a staircase in place - 19 **cabinet** a piece of furniture with glass doors used for storing small objects of interest - 22 **schooner** [ˈskuːnə] a fast sailing ship with two or more masts – 23 **sinew** [ˈsɪnjuː] a strong cord in the body connecting a muscle to a bone – **suppleness** elasticity – 26 **to account for** to give an explanation or a reason for – 29 **fluent** *here:* easy; uninterrupted – **usurper** [juːzɜːpə] a person who seizes power or a position for himself unlawfully or by force – **disreputable** [dɪsˈrepjʊtəbl] person who has a bad character – 30 **to do s.o. down** to destroy s.o. – 39 **Laugh your bloody head off!** Laugh yourself silly!

70 9 **Bound to be.** Must be, of necessity. – 12 **kith and kin** friends and relatives – 18 **proximity** nearness – 23 **with express intention** with the special intention – 36 **drive** a private road to a house – 37 **to skip** to move with quick steps and jumps – 38 **to bounce** to move up and down like a rubber ball – 39 **guffaw** [gʌˈfɔː] a loud and rude laugh – **belly laugh** a guffaw – 40 **to catch one's breath** to stop breathing for a moment as if surprised or shocked

71 4 **grief** deep sorrow – 5 **plight** bad condition or state – 10 **germ** [dʒɜːm] small living thing which causes diseases – 15 **deficiency** [dɪˈfɪʃnsɪ] imperfection – **air** *here (rare):* gentle wind, a breeze – 16 **current** continuously moving mass of air – 17 **to obtain** *here:* to exist – 18 **to quiver** to tremble – 19 **heat-haze** optical distortion caused by rising hot air – 20 **to compose o.s.** to calm o.s. down – **cranny** a hidden or little-known place – 23 **nook** a sheltered and private place – 25 **petals** [ˈpetlz] the leaf-like (often coloured) divisions of a flower – **to flake** to fall off in little pieces – 26 **foliage** [ˈfəʊlɪɪdʒ] all the leaves on a tree – 27 **to remark** to say *or:* to notice – 32 **to swirl** to move with twisting turns – 33 **to scythe** [saɪð] to cut with a long, curved knife; *here:* blades of grass touching one another – 35 **nausea** [ˈnɔːsjə] a feeling of sickness or disgust – **to rock** to move to and fro – **to gasp** to struggle for breath with the mouth open – 36 **to heave** *(of the chest):* to rise and fall regularly

72 6 **stripling** young man – 7 **to lick s.o.** to defeat s.o. – 10 **flatly** in a dull voice – **to glisten** [ˈglɪsn] to shine like something polished

Interpretation

First Unit: The Structure of the Play (with special regard to its original conception as a radio play)

Preliminary remark: For the first unit, the pupils have been asked to read the text on their own, to try and subdivide the play into scenes and to study the time and place(s) of these scenes.

77

1. Who are the characters of the play? The characters are Edward, his wife Flora, and a matchseller, who remains anonymous.

2. What information do we get about the outward appearance and the status of the three persons and how do we get this information? It is only from Edward's and Flora's descriptions that we know that the matchseller is rather old (p.55, l.3), wears a balaclava, which, as it were, masks his identity (p.61, l.39), and a dirty jersey (p.67, l.8), which makes him smelly (p.59, l.4), and that he carries a tray of matchboxes (p.54, l.32), from which we may conclude that he is a matchseller.
There is no information given about the age of the couple (we may assume that they are middle-aged) or their outward appearance, but they do give us some information about themselves when they talk to each other or to the matchseller. Edward tells the stranger that he writes "theological and philosophical essays" (p.60, l.24) as well as essays on "tropical phenomena" (p.60, ll.26f), which gives us the impression that he is an educated man – an impression strengthened by Edward's hint at his thesis (p.61, l.23), but seemingly incompatible with his statements "I was in commerce ..." (p.61, l.20) and "... I used to be in commerce" (p.62, l.14).
Flora tells the matchseller that she was a "Justice of the Peace for the county" (p.66, l.20); in the play, however, her role is that of a housewife. The couple seems to be well-off, as is suggested by the country house "full of curios" (p.58, l.29) and the well-kept garden mentioned in the stage directions at the beginning of the play.
Unlike Edward and Flora, the matchseller does not talk about himself; in fact, during the entire play he does not utter a single word! He is characterized only by others, whereas Edward and Flora characterize themselves through their words and actions.

3. Why is the fact that the matchseller is characterized by the other persons so important for A Slight Ache in its original conception as a radio play? For the spectators of the stage play, the matchseller is a character whom they can see, whereas for anyone listening to the radio play, the matchseller is virtually non-existent because he never speaks. The listener would not even know what the matchseller is like, if it were not for Edward's and Flora's descriptions as they watch the stranger and talk about or to him.

4. What are the place and time of the play? A Slight Ache is set in several rooms of a country house – the breakfast room, scullery and the study; a small part of the action takes place in the garden (see the stage directions at the beginning of the play). The action takes place one Saturday in summer (p.51, ll.19–22); it starts in the morning (cf. p.50, l.21 and p.54, ll.32f: "... at half past nine in the morning") and ends possibly in the evening (p.68, l.4: "Good evening to you." p.72, l.10: "The pool must be glistening. In the moonlight."). Whereas it appears to Edward to be evening, however, Flora tells the matchseller that he can have lunch in the garden (p.72, ll.21f). The treatment of time, then, is rather vague and open to more than one interpretation.

Apart from mentioning the "breakfast table", Pinter does not give any specific definition of time in the stage directions; instead it is Edward's and Flora's speeches which contain indications about the time.

5. A Slight Ache was originally conceived as a radio play. How did the listeners know about the different settings for the action? Someone listening to the radio play knows where the action is taking place only by indications and hints in Edward's and Flora's speeches. The remarks "Pass the teapot, please" (p.51, l.2) and "Cover the marmalade" (p.51, l.23), combined with the information on time (p.50, l.21), suggest that they are sitting at the breakfast table. Noises like the rustling of the newspaper or the rattling of teacups contribute to this impression.

Flora's question, "Edward, what are you doing in the scullery?" (p.55, ll.29f) is a clear indication of a change of scene. And the fact that, a few minutes later, Flora is talking to the matchseller in the garden is evident from her invitation: "Would you like to come inside for a little while?" (p.58, l.22).

When Flora tells her husband that the matchseller has come into the house, Edward says, "I smelt him when he came under my window" (p.59, l.6); so the room they are in must be Edward's study. The scene between Flora's announcement of the matchseller's arrival and the first meeting between Edward and the stranger takes place in the hall (cf. p.59, l.3). After his first long "conversation" with the matchseller, Edward asks to be taken into the garden (p.64, l.1), where Flora makes him sit under the canopy. Then Flora leaves him to join the matchseller, who has stayed in the study; her polite question, "Do you mind if I come in?" (p.65, l.31) tells us so. Edward's study is the setting for the rest of the play, including Edward's second "conversation" with the matchseller (with Flora not present) and Flora's return at the very end.

6. What methods does the radio play use to suggest the movements of the characters to the listener? The listener is informed about the movements the characters make by a) various sounds and noises, e.g. the sound of tea being poured into a cup (p.51, l.3), the rustling of newspaper pages (p.52, l.6), footsteps when a person enters or leaves the room, the reduced volume of Edward's and Flora's voices when they are in the garden, in the hall or just going into a room, a thud when the matchseller's tray falls down (p.62, l.18), etc.; b) Edward's and Flora's remarks: Edward's words "What is it, damn you. You're shivering. You're sagging, Come here, come here ... There. Sit here ... You're sat. At last." (p.63, ll.26–30) enable the listener to imagine the matchseller's fainting spell.

7. *Look up the definition of "scene" and try to subdivide the play into scenes.* A scene is a division of a play, usually comprising a short line of action. The end of a scene is usually indicated either by a change of place or by the exit of a character. A new scene starts when a new character comes onto the stage, when there is a change of place, or a break in the continuity of time between the new line of action and the action of the previous scene. With this in mind, we can establish a scenic structure of *A Slight Ache.*

Blackboard

(E = Edward, F = Flora, ms = matchseller)

<table>
<tr><th>No.</th><th>from – to</th><th>place</th><th>time</th><th>persons present</th></tr>
<tr><td>1</td><td>p.50, l.1 – p.55, l.26</td><td>breakfast room</td><td>morning</td><td>E, F</td></tr>
<tr><td>2</td><td>p.55, l.27 – p.58, l.13</td><td>scullery</td><td>noon</td><td>E, F</td></tr>
<tr><td>3</td><td>p.58, l.14 – p.58, l.38</td><td>garden</td><td>noon</td><td>F, ms</td></tr>
<tr><td>4</td><td>p.59, l.1 – p.59, l.27</td><td>study</td><td>noon</td><td>E, F</td></tr>
<tr><td>5</td><td>p.59, l.28 – p.59, l.34</td><td>hall</td><td>noon</td><td>F, ms</td></tr>
<tr><td>6</td><td>p.59, l.35 – p.64, l.2</td><td>study</td><td>noon</td><td>E, ms</td></tr>
<tr><td>7</td><td>p.64, l.3 – p.65, l.31</td><td>garden</td><td>noon</td><td>E, F</td></tr>
<tr><td>8</td><td>p.65, l.32 – p.67, l.30</td><td>study</td><td rowspan="2">noon/ afternoon/ early evening ?</td><td>F, ms</td></tr>
<tr><td>9</td><td>p.67, l.31 – p.68, l.3</td><td>study</td><td>E, F, ms</td></tr>
<tr><td>10</td><td>p.68, l.4 – p.72, l.14</td><td>study</td><td>evening</td><td>E, ms</td></tr>
<tr><td>11</td><td>p.72, l.15 – end</td><td>study</td><td>evening (noon?)</td><td>E, F, ms</td></tr>
</table>

Homework

Study the first two scenes of the play. Try to characterize the relationship between Edward and Flora.

Second Unit: The Relationship Between Edward and Flora at the Beginning of the Play

(The cassette recording of the first scene can be played at an appropriate time during this lesson to confirm or underline certain aspects of the relationship between Edward and Flora.)

1. Summarize the scene in the breakfast room up to the moment when Edward perceives the matchseller. Edward and Flora are sitting at the breakfast table; Edward is reading a newspaper. Flora starts talking about the shrubs in their garden, but Edward is clearly not interested in what his wife is telling him: he does not even seem to be able to distinguish between the different plants that Flora mentions. Flora comments on the beautiful weather on this Saturday morning and suggests that Edward go and work in the garden – a suggestion which Edward is not enthusiastic about as he does not trust the weather ("It's very treacherous weather, you know." p.51, l.16). Then their attention focuses on a wasp that disturbs them; first, they let it climb into the marmalade pot and put the lid on. As the wasp carries on buzzing, they ponder on several possible ways of putting it to death (drowning it in the sink, letting it drown in the marmalade, taking it out on a spoon and squashing it); finally, they decide to scald it by pouring hot water down the spoon hole; this being done, Edward takes the insect out of the pot and crushes it on the table. – The wasp episode is only interrupted by a section in which Edward tells his wife that he has a slight inexplicable ache in his eyes (p.52, ll.21–32).

2. What is the function of this opening scene? On the one hand, the conversation at the breakfast table and the wasp episode are, in themselves, banal events, seemingly of little importance. On the other hand, this opening scene provides us with some information about the two characters, so that it can be considered to be a kind of "exposition".

3. Characterize the dialogue between the two persons. We get the impression that Edward is not interested in what his wife is telling and asking him: he answers most of her questions with more questions ("The what?", "Honeysuckle? Where?", "Is that honeysuckle?" p.50, ll.10, 12 and 14). This could, of course, be attributed to the fact that he is attentively reading his paper, which might also account for his absent-mindedness ("Did you say – that the convolvulus was in flower? ... But good God, you just denied there was any." p.50, ll.23, 25; "The canopy? What for?" p.51, l.12). His full interest in what is going on around him is not roused until the arrival of the wasp. Two sections of the dialogue (EDWARD: ... I thought it was japonica. FLORA: Oh, good Lord, no. EDWARD: Pass the teapot, please. p.50, l.33–p.51, l.2; FLORA: It's the height of summer today. EDWARD: Cover the marmalade. p.51, ll.22f) might lead the student to assume that there is a failure of communication between the two people because there is no apparent logical connection between Flora's remarks and Edward's replies. But we should not forget what Pinter said in a speech delivered in 1962: "We have heard many times that tired, grimy phrase: 'Failure of communication' ... and this phrase has been fixed to my work quite consistently. I believe the contrary." ("Writing for the Theatre", p. 15). But even without Pinter's statement, it is easy to see that Edward, in these responses, is merely expressing his lack of interest in Flora's words and is trying to concentrate on his breakfast (and his paper), or, in the second example, to draw Flora's attention to the wasp.

4. What does Edward's verbal behaviour towards Flora reveal about his relationship with his wife? At the beginning, Edward, who is aware of his failure to identify the different plants in his garden and of his stupid question about the purpose of the canopy, tries to justify himself: "I don't see why I should be expected to distinguish between these plants. It's not my job." (p.51, ll.4f). His remark that the fine weather is very treacherous (p.51, l.16) seems to be an excuse for his stupid question. It seems that Edward always tries to have the last word and cannot stand the thought that, in some ways, Flora is superior to him.

5. What aspects of Edward's character does the wasp episode reveal?
a) It cannot be denied that there is a streak of perversity in Edward's character. He seems to derive a great deal of pleasure from torturing the wasp. In fact, he enjoys every single moment of it, as the slow and measured way in which he shuts the wasp in the marmalade pot shows; he follows this act with a vicious laugh and the remark "Very good." (p.52, ll.1f). Furthermore, he considers death by suffocation in the marmalade a nice death for a wasp (p.52, l.19); when it tries to crawl out, he first contents himself with the thought that it will be unable to do so and then, after a "silent pause", he decides to "kill it, for goodness' sake" (p.53, l.2) – a phrase, which, in itself, is rather crude. Before putting an end to the wasp's life, he is pleased by the thought that the hot water he is going to pour down the spoon hole

will blind the wasp before scalding it to death; he punctuates the deliberate prolongation of the wasp's agony with isolated words and phrases (p.53, ll.39f). Edward finishes this "murder" by squashing the already dead insect on a plate. After this, Edward, who, at the beginning of the play, was absent-minded and not too enthusiastic about Flora's proposition that he should go and work in the garden, seems to be elated: "I think I shall work in the garden this morning ... My goodness, just look at that sky. Not a cloud." (p.54, ll.5–9). He even answers Flora's remark "What an awful experience." with "What a beautiful day it is." (p.54, l.4f). (Note the contrast in this anaphora.)

b) Edward becomes more and more aggressive towards Flora. His bullying attitude towards his wife is highlighted by his verbal violence in their argument over whether wasps bite or sting (cf. p.51, ll.31f; p.52, ll.15f; p.53, ll.5–8).

6. *What do you think of Edward's reaction to Flora's error?* The subject of the argument with Flora is so trivial that his violent outburst must be considered an over-reaction, which could be interpreted in the following way: Edward tries to assert his superiority over Flora; by bullying his wife, he tries to underline his dominance, which was in question at the beginning of the scene when he could not distinguish between clematis, honeysuckle, and japonica.

In an interview, Pinter himself referred to this type of violence in his plays as a "battle for positions":

> The world *is* a pretty violent place, it's as simple as that, so any violence in the plays comes out quite naturally. ... The violence is really only an expression of the question of dominance and subservience ... I wrote a short story a long time ago called *The Examination*, and my ideas of violence carried on from there. That short story dealt very explicitly with two people in a room having a battle of an unspecified nature, in which the question was one of who was dominant at what point and how they were going to be dominant and what tools they would use to achieve dominance and how they would try to undermine the other person's dominance ... I wouldn't call this violence so much as a battle for positions, it's a very common everyday thing. (Quoted in Rüdiger Imhof, *Harold Pinters Dramentechnik. Gestalterische Mittel im Kontext des Gesamtwerks*, Bonn 1976, p.92.).

The quarrel over the correct verb to describe the activity of a wasp is symptomatic of a relationship that seems to be characterized by everyday routine (talk about the weather, etc.), but behind which there lurks a certain tension: the couple's nerves are strained, sometimes to breaking-point (as in the quarrel over "bite" and "sting").

7. Are there any more examples of over-reaction in this scene? Edward's tendency to make a mountain out of a mole-hill is also evident in his attitude towards the insect: he calls wasps "vicious creatures" (p.53, l.29) and refers to the dead wasp as "a monster" (p.54, ll.2f).

8. Characterize Flora in the wasp episode. Flora is afraid of the wasp (she thinks it will bite her), but at the same time strangely fascinated by the insect. She observes it very carefully and constantly draws Edward's attention, which has flagged after the wasp is trapped, back to the insect – to the point where Edward reacts very harshly: "You do know I've got work to do this morning, don't you? I can't spend the whole day worrying about a wasp." (p.53, ll.15f). Flora's nagging questions make us think that she is quite naive. Her vacillation between fear and fascination and her final eagerness to have the insect killed make us suspect that there is more to Flora's character than meets the eye.

Blackboard (see next page)

Homework

1. In "Writing for the Theatre", Pinter calls the language of his plays "a language ... where under what is said, another thing is being said". Prove this statement right by showing how the relationship between Edward and Flora is presented to us. *(This homework should lead to a summary of the results of the Second Unit, and, at the same time, sharpen the students' senses for the dialogues and monologues that are to be examined in the following units.)*
2. Study the text up to p.59, l. 34.

Blackboard Scene at the breakfast table: a kind of "exposition"

I conversation about flowers, the weather

EDWARD	FLORA
	– tries to involve her husband in casual talk
– is not interested in his wife's talk, seems absent-minded	
	– seems to be quite a naive person (asks nagging questions)
– tries to domineer; always tries to have the last word (battle for positions)	

tension lurking behind the casual talk at the breakfast table

II wasp episode

EDWARD	FLORA
– displays cruelty (prolongation of the wasp's agony)	– is afraid of the wasp, yet at the same time fascinated by it
– considers the wasp "a monster" (over-reaction)	
– becomes more and more aggressive towards his wife (quarrel over "sting" or "bite") (over-reaction)	

Third Unit: The Matchseller at the Back Gate

1. What mood is Edward in after killing the wasp? Edward feels strong and – contrary to his behaviour at the breakfast table – is now eager to go and work in the garden. He even heartily appreciates the beauty of the day and the garden.

2. Why does his mood change so suddenly? He sees the matchseller, who is standing at the back gate.

3. How can we tell that the couple already knows the matchseller by sight? Edward refers to him as "he" (not "someone" or "a person") (p.54, l.17), and Flora uses the definite article: "it's the matchseller." (p.54, l.22).

4. What information are we given about the matchseller? The matchseller has been standing at the back gate of Edward's and Flora's garden for two months (p.55, l.6). Edward even suspects him of standing there all night (p.54, l.39), as no one has ever seen him arrive in the morning (p.54, ll.37f). Apparently the matchseller has not sold a single box of matches in these two months (p.55, l.15).

5. Compare Edward's and Flora's reactions to the presence of the matchseller at the back gate. Edward is extremely irritated by the matchseller's presence; he cannot see why a matchseller should be standing at his back gate in a lane which is hardly ever used (p.55, ll.15–20). The man's presence haunts Edward and makes him think that the matchseller is an "impostor", i.e. not a matchseller at all (p.57, l.30 and ll.33f: "As for the matchseller – how ridiculous to go on calling him by that title."). This "preposterous" (p.55, l.20) and "absurd" (p.57, l.21) situation makes him feel afraid (though he denies this; see p.57, ll.12–15), as is clear from his confession that, since the arrival of the matchseller, he has not dared to go past him into the lane (p.55, ll.7–13). Not knowing the identity of the matchseller worries Edward a lot. When, at the beginning of scene two, Flora comes into the scullery, he has been observing the matchseller for more than two hours (from breakfast until noon; see the time given p.56, l.2), and he can give a detailed report of the stranger's behaviour on this Saturday morning (cf. p.57, ll.22–33).
Flora is in no way surprised at the presence of the matchseller ("he's always there" p.54, l.24). For her, the matchseller is a "quiet, harmless old man" (p.55, l.22). Therefore, she cannot understand Edward's uneasiness and fear (p.55, l.21). But at the same time she herself is clearly in some way fascinated by the matchseller; her question "Do you find him interesting, Edward?" (p.55, l.1) may lead us to the assumption that *she* somehow does.

Furthermore, she seems to know at what time he arrives and has even tried to establish some form of contact with him (cf. p.54, l.34; p.55, ll.4f).

6. Try to find parallels between the couple's conversation and the scene at the breakfast table. Edward's and Flora's reactions to the presence of the matchseller can be likened to their reactions to the presence of the wasp: Edward seems to over-react to the situation, whereas Flora is in some strange way fascinated by the matchseller, just as she was by the wasp.
The matchseller's presence gives rise to a certain aggressiveness in Edward, which, again, manifests itself in his verbal behaviour, though this time it is not directed against Flora. At the very sight of the matchseller, he starts swearing (p.54, l.19), and at one point a whole sequence of his utterances consists of swear words ("Damn it", "Damn", "Damn", "Christ blast it": p.57, ll.4, 6, 8, 11). Edward's outbursts may be due both to his inability to make sense of the matchseller's presence at his back gate, but also to the fact that he is showing weakness in front of his wife.
Like the scene at the breakfast table, the couple's talk about the stranger is an example of a battle for positions. Thus Edward denies being afraid of the stranger and pretends to look for some notes in the scullery, whereas the only reason why he is in that room is that he can easily watch the matchseller from there. To establish his dominance, he tries to make Flora feel inferior by telling her of (or rather inventing) things she does not know anything about. His explanation to Flora that he is writing an essay on "the dimensionality and continuity of space ... and time" (p.56, ll.21f) and his statement that he keeps notes in the scullery can be considered as a lie and a pretext, respectively.
Edward's objection to Flora calling him "Beddie-Weddie" (p.57, l.1) can be interpreted in two ways: either he does not like to be treated like a child by Flora or he hates this nickname, which seems to be composed of "Eddie" (the short form for "Edward", "bed" and "wed" [= married]), because the sexual connotation embarrasses him.

7. What decision does Edward make at the end of the scene in the scullery? He decides to invite the matchseller into the house; by talking to him, Edward intends to "get to the bottom of it" (p.58, l.2), i.e. find out who and what the matchseller is.

8. Why does he ask Flora to invite the matchseller in? On no account does Edward want to leave his house: "Go out to *him*?. Certainly ... not. I'll invite him in here. Into my study." (p.58, ll.1f). This may sound like a refusal to condescend to leave his house in order to invite an unknown pedlar to come inside. But a few minutes earlier, Edward had already expressed his fear of leaving his house and going for a walk. From this, we may conclude that, for Edward, his house is a sort of refuge, where he feels secure. A number of critics have ascribed to the room and the interior of a house – the most frequent settings of Pinter's plays – the meaning of a "safe haven", i.e. "a small area of the known amid the vast unknown" (cf. Imhof, *op.cit.*, p.45).

9. Characterize the way in which Flora approaches the matchseller. In approaching the matchseller, Flora behaves rather awkwardly. Her speech is frequently interrupted by pauses, which are due to the matchseller's silence and her own embarrassment. After a formal greeting and the introduction of herself and her husband as the owners of the house, she invites him in for a drink. Her first suggestion ("a cup of tea") draws no response from the matchseller, which makes her suggest another drink ("a glass of lemon"). After another pause, she hints at the interest she and her husband have in the matchseller. Clearly, the sentence "There's something we'd very much like to ..." (p.58. ll.22f) can only be completed by "know". At the last moment, Flora realizes that this would mean admitting that the invitation to a drink is only a pretext and she quickly completes the sentence with "tell you, that will benefit you". The plausibility of this pretext, however, is marred by Flora's babbling about her intention to buy the tray of matches; she pretends to have run out of matches and suggests settling the sale "inside" (p.58, l.25). In addition to this, she hides her true intention by giving the matchseller the prospect of an interesting visit ("Our house is full of curios ..." p.58, ll.28f) and of a good lunch. She finally manages to take his arm and leads the stranger towards the house; in doing so, she tells the matchseller the names of the flowers in her garden and so apparently tries to live up to her promise that the visit will be interesting.

10. In what way are the short dialogue between Flora and Edward and her explanations to the matchseller (p.59, ll.1–32) further evidence for her interest in the stranger? Flora feels protective towards the matchseller. She fears that Edward will be too hard on him, perhaps even use physical violence: "What are you going to do with him, Edward? You won't be rough with him in any way?" (p.59, ll.8f). When she shows the matchseller the way to Edward's study, her indication that the door is at the top is twice interrupted by pauses, which is due to the fascination the matchseller's movements have for her (see the stage direction: "She watches him move."). The way in which he climbs the stairs literally seems to take her breath away.

Blackboard

The matchseller at the back gatc
- irritates Edward: not knowing the identity of the stranger makes him lose his self-control (swear words; battle for positions with Flora)
- makes Edward feel afraid (he doesn't leave the 'haven' of his house)
- fascinates Flora

Homework

Study scene no. 6 (p.59, l.35–p.64, l.2).

Fourth Unit: Edward's First "Conversation" With the Matchseller

1. What does Edward hope to achieve by inviting the matchseller into the house? Edward intends "to get to the bottom of it" (p.57, l.35), i.e. he wants to inquire into the identity and the activities of the matchseller, who he suspects is an "impostor" (p.57, l.30). We may therefore expect Edward to cross-examine the stranger in an effort to shed light on the identity of the old man, and to solve the mystery of his presence at the back gate.

2. Why is this examination bound to fail? The reason why Edward's efforts are not (and cannot be) successful lies in the very nature of the "talk" he has with the stranger. As the matchseller is completely silent, Edward's examination degenerates into a kind of "monologue" (or – to repeat a phrase used by some critics – "a dialogue with silence"). At the places where we expect a response from Edward's "interlocutor", we only find pauses, which make this "communication" rather a clumsy affair.

3. Study Edward's "monologue" up to the moment when the matchseller's tray falls down. Why are we surprised at Edward's first words? The cheerful tone of Edward's voice (cf. p.59, l.35) is diametrically opposed to the harshness he showed at the sight of the matchseller at the back gate. There is nothing in Edward's behaviour to justify Flora's fears. Her husband even treats the stranger as if he were an old acquaintance, as his familiar greeting, "Don't stand out there, old chap" (p.59, l.37) shows. The fact that he rises at the entry of the old man could even be taken as a sign of a certain respect for the stranger. There is absolutely no hint of Edward's original intention to cross-examine the matchseller. Of course, there might also be another reason for Edward's behaviour: by using an informal tone, he wants to reassure his guest. Edward's informal address to the stranger ("old chap"; "old man": p.60, l.4) could also be considered as a means of disguising his own nervousness; he tries to conceal the fact that the matchseller and the mystery of his identitiy worry him by treating the old man in a haughty way.

4. *Does Edward have a clearly structured strategy?* Edward does not seem to have a clear-cut strategy; his "monologue" consists of several short passages on different subjects.

5. *What are the subjects Edward touches on in his "monologue"?* They are: the former squire of the village and his lovely daughters (p.60, ll.7–15); the variety of seats in Edward's study (p.60, ll.17–21); the subjects of his essays (p.60, ll.24–35); the beauty of the village (p.60, l.37–p.61, l.2); Edward's plans for the afternoon (p.61, ll.8–12); his praise of his wife (p.61, ll.14–17); his commercial career (p.61, ll.19–26); his interest in Asia and Africa and an invitation to the matchseller to choose from a large variety of drinks (p.61, ll.28–37); his concern for the matchseller's clothes (p.61, l.39–p.62, l.1); his concern for the place where the matchseller plies his trade (p.62, ll.3–6); his suspicion that the matchseller might have a glass eye (p.62, l.8); his enquiry about the contents of the matchboxes (p.62, ll.10–14); another invitation to have a drink (p.62, ll.14–17).

6. *Try to find a logical connection between the parts of Edward's speech.* At first sight, there does not seem to be any logical connection between the different paragraphs of Edward's speech. It might, however, be said that Edward moves from one subject to the next by *association*. For example, his offer of a drink to the matchseller leads to his claim that he entertains the villagers once a year and from there to the former squire and his daughter. Similarly, his invitation to the matchseller to sit down makes him turn to the subject of the various chairs he uses when he is working and to the wide variety of themes he claims to be working on. The fact that "maps" (p.60, l.34) are his only way of exploring the world is related to Edward's confession: "I don't often go down [to the village], of course." (p.60, l.37), which shows us Edward's seclusion from the world outside as well as his tendency to study problems from an exclusively theoretical point of view. The remaining parts of Edward's monologue up to the moment when the tray falls down are much less coherent, which could be due to Edward's increasing confusion.

7. *Are there any passages in Edward's speech in which he pursues his original intention?* Edward's monologue is interspersed here and there with questions that are meant to inquire into the matchseller's past and present situations (cf. p.60, ll.14f; 28–30, 37f; p.62, ll.3f). His questions are promp-

ted by the subjects he has just touched upon. It is not clear whether they merely come into his mind as he is talking or whether there is some specific strategy behind this that consists in the apparently arbitrary inclusion of questions within an informal conversation intended to reassure the matchseller. The first explanation seems the more likely.

8. In what way does the matchseller's silence influence Edward's speech? Edward's speech becomes increasingly confused; the frequent changes of subject may be due to his attempt to find some stimulus which might make the matchseller react to what he is saying. As this proves a complete failure, Edward becomes more and more embarrassed and has to struggle for words and subjects, which is demonstrated

a) by the pauses that interrupt his speech, dividing it into different sections;

b) by some pauses he has to make within these sections and which are indicated by dots (cf. p.61, ll.19f, 21–24);

c) by the repetition of words and phrases. Example: "Often when I'm working, you know, I draw up one chair, scribble a few lines, put it by, draw up another, sit back, ponder, put it by ... *(absently)* ... sit back ... put it by ... (p.60, ll.19–20). His abrupt stop after saying "flaming red hair" (p.61, l.17) might be interpreted as his sudden realization that he used exactly the same words only a few minutes before (see p.60, l.11).;

d) by his use of platitudes and commonplaces for lack of subjects and appropriate words. Example: "Get a good woman to stick by you. Never mind what the world says. Keep at it. Keep your shoulder to the wheel. It'll pay dividends." (p.61, ll.24–26);

e) by his answering his own questions to the matchseller or providing replies to imaginary questions or statements (cf. p.61, ll.9f; p.62, ll.4–6). (This strange sequence of questions and answers, with which Edward obviously tries to compensate for the total lack of verbal interaction with the old man, can also be found *after* the matchseller's tray falls down: cf. p.63, ll.11–14; 18–20).

9. What does Edward reveal about his own character in his "dialogue with silence"? The first characteristic trait that becomes evident is Edward's conceitedness. At the very beginning of his speech, he asserts his superiority by claiming that the villagers look upon him "with some regard" (p.60, l.8), though this might seem strange when seen in the light of his deliberate seclusion from the village ("I don't often go down, of course." p.60, l.37). When talking about his essays, he fires strange-sounding geographical names at the matchseller, two of which do not even exist (Membunza Mountains, Katambaloo), only to reveal that he owes his knowledge of

these regions to having studied maps ("Never been there myself. Studied the maps though." p.60, ll.34f). Edward even considers himself partly responsible for the beauty of the village: "*We* win the first prize regularly, you know, the best kept village in the area" (p.60, l.39–p.61, l.1). Given the fact that he lives outside the village, this statement can only be called pretentious.
Edward claims to have been "in commerce" (p.61, l.20; p.62, l.14) and to be familiar with the difficulties the job of a travelling salesman implies (cf. p.61, ll.21–23). What he has to say about his career as a salesman, however, is hardly compatible with the remark "up till all hours working at your thesis" (p.61, l.23).
Edward offers the stranger an astonishing variety of exotic drinks (cf. p.61, ll.33–37), but in the end recommends an ordinary "glass of cider" (p.62, l.16).
By using French words like "petit déjeuner" and "apéritif" (p.62, l.15), Edward obviously tries to show off his education (as he does when quoting at length the names of German wines). Unfortunately, he doesn't know *how* to use these expressions: "petit déjeuner" means "breakfast", not "lunch", and on no account can cider be considered an aperitif.
Thus it can be said that in his monologue Edward turns out to be himself the "impostor" he saw in the matchseller (cf. p.57, l.30).

10. How can Edward's imposture be explained? There are at least two possible explanations: a) Edward is merely trying to win the matchseller's admiration and respect – something he is normally denied because of his isolation. b) We can consider the "examination" as just another "battle for positions", in which Edward tries to make his stand, i.e. to demonstrate his superiority over the matchseller. – These two interpretations, different as they may be, point to the fact that Edward lacks self-confidence. Trying to impress the old matchseller can only be considered as an attempt to surmount his inferiority complex.

11. Describe the change in Edward's behaviour after the tray falls down. After this incident, Edward really gets "down to brass tacks" (p.63, ll.9f): he gives up his sanctimonious politeness and reveals the true intention behind his conversation with the matchseller: "No doubt you're wondering why I invited you into this house?" (p.63, l.12). He even comes up with the question that has been nagging at him for so long: "Why do you stand outside my back gate, from dawn till dusk, why do you pretend to sell matches, why ...?" (p.63, ll.24–26). Not only does he openly accuse the old man of being an impostor, he also admits his disgust at the matchseller (cf.

p.63, ll.15f). He does not even hesitate to characterize the matchseller's mental abilities in words that are anything but polite: "... I had decided that you had the comprehension of a bullock." (p.63, ll.6f). But even in these moments of apparent frankness, he does not always tell the truth. His statement, "I did not find you at all alarming. No, no. Nothing outside this room has ever alarmed me." (p.63, ll.14/15) is at variance with his over-reaction to the appearance both of the matchseller and of the wasp. This obvious lie can be considered as another move in his "battle for positions" with the stranger, but it only strengthens our impression that Edward has an inferiority complex, which he endeavours to camouflage behind a mask of self-confidence built on deception and imposture.

12. What may have caused the change in Edward's behaviour? Obviously, the fall of the tray and the observation this incident allows Edward to make play an important role: the fact that the matches are wet, i.e. cannot possibly serve any reasonable purpose, seems to corroborate Edward's assertion that the old man is an impostor. This realization and the total failure of his efforts to elicit a reaction from the matchseller goad Edward into addressing himself openly to the stranger rather than wasting time beating about the bush. By asking pointed questions, Edward hopes to force the old man to stop resisting and to admit everything Edward accuses him of.

13. What incident puts an end to Edward's "examination"? Just as Edward is asking the matchseller why he has been standing at the garden gate, the old man has a fainting spell (cf. p.63, l.26 und l.28). At first sight, it seems as if the matchseller breaks down under the strain of Edward's direct and uncompromising questioning. On the other hand, his fainting may simply be due to the heat and to the fact that he has been standing ever since he entered the room. Strangely enough, Edward does not attempt to profit from the matchseller's faint by asking further embarrassing questions, but is really shocked by the man's breakdown.
The old man's collapse has a strange parallel in Edward's exhaustion of a few moments later: "I must get some air. I must get a breath of air." (p.63, l.37). Edward's fatigue may be due to the fact that he finds himself at his wit's end after the questioning and his endeavour to discover the matchseller's identity – at least for the time being.

14. What is striking about the last subject Edward touches on – the purchase of his furniture? After his statement that he bought all his furniture in the same sale when still a young man, Edward makes an enigmatic remark: "You too, perhaps. You too, perhaps. ... At the same time, perhaps!"

(p.63, ll.33–35). It seems as if the presence of the matchseller and the mystery of his identity haunt Edward to the point where he desperately tries to find an experience he might have shared with the old man in the past. This nonsensical attempt verges on the neurotic (and prepares us for Edward's breakdown at the end of his second "conversation" with the matchseller).

Edward's remark may also be interpreted in the following manner: Edward tries to project his own identity onto the old man, seeing in him a double, as it were. A first hint at this identification is given earlier: "I was in much the same position myself then as you are now ..." (p.61, l.19). When looking at the matchseller Edward seems to see himself, which would also explain his own faint so soon after the matchseller's collapse.

Blackboard

Edward's "conversation" with the matchseller → the matchseller's complete silence
(original intention: cross-examination)

FAILURE

Edward gives more information about himself than he gets from the matchseller.

↓

degenerates into a monologue (a "dialogue with silence"), which displays
- Edward's conceitedness and imposture (in another "battle for positions")
- Edward's inferiority complex
- Edward's increasing confusion as to the identity of the matchseller
- Edward's recognition of the matchseller as his double

FAILURE of Edward's original intention

↓

Edward's breakdown (physical and mental exhaustion) at the end of the scene

Homework

1. Suppose the matchseller is really a harmless old pedlar. Try to imagine his thoughts during Edward's speech. *(Teacher: Here, the pupils are asked to produce some imaginative writing of their own. Of course, this homework also means reproducing some of the results of the work in the Fourth Unit: it should include the matchseller's total ignorance of the reason why he has been invited, his uneasiness, his disgust at Edward's conceitedness, his surprise at Edward's questions, etc. Any suggestion that does not contain elements that run counter to the possibilities offered by the text should be critically accepted.)*
2. Study scenes 7–9 (p.64, l.3–p.68, l.3).

Fifth Unit: Flora's Role in Scenes 7–9

1. Characterize the atmosphere of the dialogue between Flora and her husband. At the beginning of the dialogue, the atmosphere between Edward and Flora is marked by a sort of peaceful togetherness: Flora leads her husband out into the garden, and the worried and exhausted Edward gladly accepts his wife's tender care; she reassures him by making him aware of the familiar sights and sounds of the garden. She even offers to bring Edward's lunch out into the garden, so that he can enjoy it in peace. The quarrel they had before the matchseller entered the house seems to be forgotten. But the dialogue soon turns into a bitter argument between the two people.

2. What causes this sudden change in atmosphere? We might say it is the matchseller who is "responsible" for the resurgence of verbal violence between the couple. As soon as Flora starts inquiring into the outcome of the conversation between Edward and the matchseller, her husband reacts sharply ("What do you mean?" p.64, l.17), preparing the reader for the ensuing quarrel.

3. Before the quarrel with Flora, however, Edward characterizes the matchseller. Interpret this passage. It seems surprising that Edward should be able to characterize the stranger, as the old man has not said a word. Nevertheless, Edward claims to have found out some facts about him ("A little. A little." p.64, l.23). By emphasizing that the matchseller was reticent and withdrawn, he underlines his own capacity for getting information out of the old man. But his pretence is at least partially belied by the "conclusions" he arrives at: it soon becomes clear that his only evidence is the matchseller's silence, which he interprets at will. The fact that Edward's questions, "Do you live in the village? ... Or are you passing through?" (p.60, ll.37f) elicit no reaction from the matchseller certainly cannot justify the statement that his "place of residence is unsure" (p.64, ll.23f), just as the fact that the old man meets Edward's offer of a drink with silence does not warrant the conclusion that "he's not a drinking man" (p.64, l.24). Obviously, Edward tries everything to make his wife believe that the matchseller actually talked to him, in an endeavour to conceal the shameful truth that his "cross-examination" proved to be a complete failure. Edward's conversation with his wife is thus another instance of a "battle for positions". This is also underlined by his confident claim that he will find out the reason for the matchseller's arrival "by nightfall" (p.64, ll.25f).

4. Does Edward succeed in fooling his wife? Obviously, Flora knows Edward well enough to realize that the matchseller and the mystery of his identity still worry her husband a lot. She even anticipates one possible reason for his interest in the matchseller: she thinks that Edward may consider the old man to be part of a plot against him ("... he's not here through any ... design, or anything ...: p.64, ll.31f). She tries to assuage her husband's fears by assuring him that the matchseller is really quite harmless, just "an old man, weak in the head" (p.64, ll.34f). Edward, however, is not prepared to accept his wife's opinion. In a desperate attempt to deny his fear of the stranger and to prove his wife wrong (and so to justify his reaction to the matchseller), he points out the stranger's physical disabilities (i.e. his obesity, his defective eyesight, his deafness and his exhaustion). But in doing so, he only supports his wife's arguments.

Flora, too, seems to sense that the stranger is a potential danger, not necessarily to her, but to her husband. For the second time she suggests to Edward that they should make the stranger move on, give up his position at the back gate (p.64, l.33; she wants to use her own power of persuasion this time, but had suggested force earlier on; cf. p.58, ll.10f).

5. Interpret Edward's reaction to Flora's intention of speaking to the matchseller. Edward reacts violently, dropping his mask of complacency ("And I know he knows I know it." p.65, l.10). Not only does the presence of the matchseller upset him, but now he even suspects Flora of plotting against him or of acting in collusion with the matchseller. (His question, "What are you plotting?" p.65, ll.20, 25, is ambiguous, as *you* can refer to Flora alone or to Flora and the matchseller).

In this quarrel between Edward and Flora, the "battle for positions" takes on a wider significance. It is no longer a battle on a merely personal level, but becomes a battle between the sexes. Flora counters Edward's derogatory affirmation "... you're a woman, you know nothing" (p.65, l.7) with the assertion "A woman ... a woman will often succeed, you know, where a man must invariably fail." (p.65, ll.29f).

Moreover, she reproaches him with being heavy-handed, "in every way" (p.65, l.27), which, apart from being a hint at Edward's treatment of the matchseller, might also be an allusion to Edward's inability to give her sexual satisfaction. This might be important, when seen in the light of the episode in which Flora confronts the matchseller.

The fact that Edward ceases protesting about Flora's plan may be due to his wife's powers of persuasion or simply to Edward's realization that after his own failure, he can only hope to get at the truth with Flora's help.

6. How does Flora start her conversation with the stranger (p.65, l.32–p.66, l.3)? What does this tell us about Flora? Flora's question, "Do you mind if I come in?", displays a certain respect for the matchseller. She starts her conversation with almost the same question she asked her husband at the beginning of the play ("It's the longest day of the year today, did you know that?" p.65, l.36). But then she goes on to talk about the terrible weather of a few months before (the frost, the floods). Although this may simply be a thought association with her preceding sentence, it might be said that Flora displays an almost complete lack of a sense of reality. As to her original intention of cross-examining the matchseller, the only sentence that has the value of a question is "I hope you weren't here in the floods." (p.65, l.38).

The subject of the deliberate seclusion from the outside world that is touched upon in Edward's first "conversation" with the matchseller (cf. p.60, l.37) is taken up by Flora: the location of their house on a hill protected them from the floods (and so meant security for them). But Flora even seems to derive a sense of romanticism from their isolation: the house was an island, as it were ("The country was a lake. Everything stopped.": p.66, l.2), where she and Edward could live independently of the world around them and escape reality ("... studied other cultures." p.66, l.3). This sort of escape and Flora's fantasies become even more prominent in the following passages.

7. Study p.66, l.5 to p.67, l.29. What is the relationship Flora tries to establish between herself and the matchseller? What does Flora's speech tell us about her relationship with Edward?

Note on procedure: These two questions can be dealt with in group work; the teacher should give each group the same questions, allowing them some

20–30 minutes. Results should then be discussed in the classroom.

1) In the main part of Flora's "dialogue" with the stranger, it becomes evident why she is so fascinated with the matchseller. She tells him that he reminds her of a poacher who raped her when she was still in her youth ("It was my first canter unchaperoned." p.66, ll.17f). She recalls every detail of this experience and is even able to relate it in rather a dramatic style (note the short sentences and clauses p.66, ll.9–13). The fact that she can relate the "desperate battle" with such composure shows that this experience has not led to a trauma. She even manages to find some sort of an excuse for it by blaming the times ("... life was perilous in those days": p.66, l.17).

Obviously, Flora considers the matchseller not only a look-alike of the man who raped her, but the criminal himself. She clearly associates the body odour of the poacher with the vile smell of the matchseller: "A bit of a stinker. (Pause) I say, you are perspiring, aren't you? Shall I mop your brow?" (p.66, ll.24–26). The fact that the rape took place on a muddy cattle track ("Up to my ears in mud." p.66, l.13) leads her to associate the dirty clothes of the matchseller (cf. p.67, ll.8–10) with the clothes of the poacher, obviously filthy from rolling in the mud with her. Inquiring into the matchseller's interest in sex, she hesitantly asks him: "Have you ever ... stopped a woman?" (p.66, l.36). Obviously, this question is to serve the purpose of making the old man admit that *he* was the person who, by a clever ruse, stopped her during her canter along the hillside cattle track.

But this "realization" that the stranger is the man who raped her is far from filling Flora with disgust or even fear; the very thought that she shared a sexual experience with the old man makes her work herself up "into sexual excitement about him" (Martin Esslin, *Pinter. A Study of His Plays*, London 1970, p.89). She tries to seduce the old man, as becomes evident from the stage directions: "She leans on the arm of chair" and starts talking "intimately" (p.66, ll.33f) about sex. She tries to find out about his interest in sex; the matchseller's silence does not deter her from continuing to talk about this. The juxtaposition of the two sentences, "Does it ever occur to you that sex is a very vital experience *for other people?* Really, I think you'd amuse *me* if you weren't so hideous." (p.67, ll.1–3), is the clearest demonstration of her interest in the stranger as a sexual partner. Her desires are underlined by her seductive tone of voice (cf. p.67, l.4) and her imagining that the matchseller is whispering obscenities to her (cf. p.67, l.6), and she finally proceeds to undress the stranger: "And what have you got under your jersey? Let's see... I'm not tickling you, am I?" (p.67, ll.10f). Other steps taken by Flora in order to arouse the stranger sexually are: her compliments on his (solid) body (p.67, ll.14f), her intention of giving him a scrub (p.67, ll.15f), and finally her passionate embrace ("She throws her arms round him." p.67, l.16).

It is evident that Flora's sexual frustration has its origins in her marriage. Her dissatisfaction with her sex life sheds a new light on her remark to Edward in the previous scene: "You're much too heavy-handed, *in every way.*" (p.65, ll.26f). In saying this, she seems to be reproaching him with his incompetence as a lover (see also above, Third Unit, section 6). It would be fair to say, therefore, that Flora's sexual interest in the matchseller is an indirect criticism of her boring love life, for which she blames her husband. She gathers strength and self-confidence from the matchseller, whose presence kindles her dormant sexuality. Thus she relishes the thought that she is the reason for the matchseller's perspiring, which she interprets as a reaction to her presence (cf. p.66, ll.26f; note the ambiguity of *closeness* which can either refer to the stifling air or to their being close to one another).

The theme of sexuality in connection with the matchseller has been introduced very early in the play. Looking out of the scullery window, Flora identifies the matchseller as a bullock: "Is that a bullock let loose? No. It's the matchseller!" (p.56, ll.28f). The word "bullock" carries two meanings, which, in this context, are opposites: a bullock may be "a young bull" and hence a symbol of sexual potency, or "a steer, a castrated bull", i.e. the very opposite of potency. When Edward takes over Flora's description of the matchseller ("... standing like a bullock ... a bullock, outside my back gate." p.57, ll.36f), it becomes clear that he sees a sexual rival in him. When he refers to the matchseller as a bullock later on (p.63, l.7; p.65, l.4), he seems to have the other meaning in mind.

2) For Flora the matchseller is not only a substitute for Edward as a sexual partner, he also embodies the romantic lover, a sort of Prince Charming. Whereas her husband believes that the matchseller's presence at his back gate is part of a plot against him, Flora sees in the old man a person who is in love with her and has followed her to her home and woos her by timidly standing at her back gate: "You've been standing waiting for me. You've seen me in the woods, picking daisies, in my apron, my pretty daisy apron, and you came and stood, poor creature, at my gate, till death us do part." (p.67, ll.22–25). The inclusion of part of the pledge from the marriage ceremony is another hint at Flora's unfulfilled dream of a husband, who, unlike Edward, will make her happy for the rest of her life. It can also be read as an expression of her wish that Edward should die and that the matchseller should take his place.

It should be pointed out here that Flora's imagination runs amok: given her beautiful garden, it seems highly unlikely that she ever picked daisies in the woods. Flora seems to assume the role of a girl from a fairytale, a mixture of Little Red Riding Hood and Snow-White. This could also make us doubt the truth of the story of her rape; Esslin asserts that "the encounter with the old matchseller provokes Flora into the sexual *fantasies* of her youth about *possible* first, unchaperoned "canters" and being set upon by "wild men" (*op. cit.* p.89). Whether the events Flora relates are true or not, it is incontestable that the matchseller's presence ignites Flora's desire for a sexually adequate partner as well as a man who is ready to adore and woo her even after many years of routine marital life – expectations which Edward has not lived up to.

3) Flora's attitude towards the old man is not only one of unrestrained sexuality, but also one of almost maternal protectiveness. At the end of her speech she imagines how she will coddle the matchseller – "I'm going to put you to bed. I'm going to put you to bed and watch over you ... And I'll buy you pretty little things that will suit you. And little toys to play with." (p.67, ll.25–28) – a fantasy that might be due to her being denied a child of her own. From the previous scenes, we know that Edward is not ready to assume the role of a child and that he rejects all her attempts to coddle him. Flora thinks that she has found a child surrogate in the matchseller.

Flora's obsession with the thought of having found a person who incorporates all her desires and dreams shows itself a) in the frequent repetition of words and phrases and the brevity of her sentences, showing excitement; b) in the confusion in the last paragraph of her speech. After assigning the role of Prince Charming to the matchseller (p.67, ll.22–25) and immediately going on to offer him the comforts that are normally given to a child (ll.25–28), she suddenly mentions the subject of death, which gives rise to a strange juxtaposition of sentences: "And little toys to play with. On your deathbed. Why shouldn't you die happy?" (p.67, ll.27–29). At this moment, Flora seems no longer able to distinguish between her fantasies (the role of a child that her imagination would like the old man to assume) and reality (the old age of the matchseller and, as a consequence, his possible imminent death). She exaggerates the old man's pathetic condition to the point where she even wants to make Edward believe that the old man is about to die, which draws an angry diatribe from her husband ("You lying slut." p.67, l.39). In fact, Edward cannot but interpret Flora's wild statements as a pretext for keeping him out of the room so that he shall not see that she has actually started undressing the matchseller. [It should be noted that Edward considers the matchseller to be younger than does his wife: "He's not dying! Nowhere near. He'll see you cremated." (p.67, l.37). This might prove important in the last part of the play, in which Edward thinks he notices a gradual rejuvenation of the stranger.]

8. Does Flora's interaction with the matchseller in any way serve the purpose of disclosing the old man's identity? Flora's original intention ("I can find out all about him", p.65, l.13) is contradicted by the result of her "conversation" with the matchseller; possibly, her attempt to solve the mystery of the old man's identity was merely a pretext, on which she tried to be alone with the stranger in order to seduce him and to flaunt her sexuality. The critic Arnold P. Hinchliffe has this to say about Flora's view of the matchseller's identity: "For Flora, the problem of who or what the matchseller is is soon settled – she gives the matchseller a name, Barnabas ...*; and, in naming him, she solves the problem of his identity. Barnabas becomes for her the desirable and submissive combination of child, husband, and lover that the apparently dominant Edward never could be." Hinchliffe, *Harold Pinter*, New York 1967, p.69). *(Teacher: At this point in the discussion, the teacher should introduce the term "the catalytic stranger", which a number of critics regard as one of the most important motifs in Pinter's plays. "The catalytic stranger" is a figure that intrudes or is invited into an apparently well-ordered world. The confrontation between the inhabitants of this world and the stranger leads to the crumbling of all façades, uncovering a host of frustrations that lurk behind them. Faced with the matchseller, Flora is forced to strip away layer after layer of her complacent existence; the old man is a catalyst whose presence makes Flora reveal her true nature and make the matchseller the object of her pent-up desires.)*

* The name Barnabas occurs in the Bible (Acts 4, 36): "... Joses, who by the apostles was surnamed Barnabas, (which is, being interpreted, The son of consolation,) ..." We may say, then, that Flora considers the matchseller a source of consolation and names him accordingly.

Blackboard

Flora's confrontation with the matchseller

(original intention: solve the mystery of the old man's identity)

↓

betrayal of the original intention

↑

Flora's behaviour →	*The roles Flora's fantasy would like the old man to assume* →	*indirect criticism of her husband*
– unrestrained sexuality	– lover, sexual partner	– Edward's impotence
– her adoration of the matchseller	– "Prince Charming"	– the boring routine of her marital life with Edward
– her maternal protectiveness	– child	– Edward's refusal to be coddled

the combination of Flora's desires and unsatisfied needs; "the son of consolation"

↓

The matchseller is a "catalyst" whose presence makes Flora become aware of and exhibit freely her true self; he provides a disturbing insight into the complexities of Flora's character and the host of frustrations lurking behind the apparently peaceful façade of family life.

Homework

1. Give a portrayal of Flora's emotional life as it becomes apparent in her "conversation" with the matchseller. *(Teacher: This homework consists of a retrospective assessment of Flora's emotional development; in doing it, the pupils should make ample use of the results of Unit Five. They should reorganize the clues in the text and their interpretation into an essay dealing with the three main stages of Flora's development: 1) the rape scene, 2) her marriage with Edward, 3) her encounter with the matchseller. Further details about the second stage might be provided by the preceding units, so that this homework enables a) the pupils to integrate the results of the previous lessons into the new findings of Unit Five, b) the teacher to make the pupils recapitulate the results of the previous lessons, which will be important for the interpretation of Edward's second encounter with the matchseller.)*

2. Study the rest of the text. Try to find parallels between Edward's first encounter with the matchseller and his second "conversation" with the old man. Make a note of the differences between the two scenes, with special regard to Edward's behaviour.

3. Do you think that temporary marriage could be a remedy for frustrations such as those experienced by Flora?

Sixth Unit: Edward's Second "Conversation" With the Matchseller

1. *Study the beginning of Edward's second "conversation" with the matchseller (up to p.69, l.9). Compare his tone of voice with that at the beginning of the first "conversation".* Whereas Edward started his first "dialogue with silence" in a cheerful tone of voice (cf. p.59, l.35), he is not as friendly at the beginning of his second conversation with the stranger (cf. *"coolly"*: p.68, l.4). This change in atmosphere may be due to the event preceding this scene, namely Flora's attempted seduction of the old man; this has probably confirmed Edward in his suspicion that the matchseller and Flora are part of a plot against him.

2. *Does the change in Edward's tone of voice imply any changes in his intentions and methods of questioning?* No, it does not. The fact that he is still determined to discover the identity of the matchseller is evidenced by the inclusion of questions that are clearly meant to inquire into the matchseller's past (cf. p.68, ll.19, 37f). As in the first conversation, the match-

seller's silence leads Edward to answer his own questions ("More comfortable? Yes." p.68, l.11) or at least to suggest possible replies (p.68, ll.21f: "What did you do with it? Run? Swim? Kick the ball? You kicked the ball? What position? Left back? Goalie? First reserve?"). His speech reveals a certain amount of conceitedness (he claims to have been wicket keeper for his team, which also requires good batting skills). Again, he tries to create stimuli to which the matchseller could respond (e.g. the mention of Cavendish). Again, his patience proves to be short-lived. Faced with the failure of his efforts and the matchseller's silence, which he interprets as a deliberate opposition to his questions, Edward's temper explodes ("God damn it...": p.68, l.38). Due to the fact that the stranger is on his "territory" (p.68, l.39) and has shared his food and drink, Edward thinks he has the right to know everything about him. [It is not clear whether the matchseller has actually accepted Edward's offer of a drink and has eaten of the goose (which Edward refers to as "duck") Flora prepared for lunch (cf. p.58, l.30). If he has, this is just another example of the radio play imparting part of the action through the words of (one of) the characters. If the matchseller has not touched any of the food and drink, which is much more probable, this passage must be interpreted as pure imagination and wishful thinking. Edward would like to have arguments to back up his desperate quest for the matchseller's identity; as there aren't any, Edward finds himself stripped of any power over the stranger and invents evidence on which his claim can be founded.]

3. In what way is the beginning of Edward's second conversation with the matchseller a logical sequel to the last paragraph of his first conversation (cf. p.63, ll.31–35)? At the end of his first conversation with the matchseller, Edward tried to attain his goal by reminding the stranger of an experience he might have shared with him. The words he used then can almost be seen as the beginning of a hesitant identification with the matchseller. This impression is strengthened by the use of the pronouns "we/us" at the beginning of Edward's second speech ("Let'*s* open these window, then ..." and "Don't want to suffocate, do *we*?" p.68, l.9; italics added). The fact that the process of Edward's identification with the matchseller has already been initiated makes another passage take on an ambiguous meaning. Edward's remarks, "Make yourself at home. Do as you would in your own house". (p.68, ll.12f) are not only cliché-like invitations, which are common for a host. They are, like Edward's remark to Flora in scene 7 ("I should be the same, perhaps, in his place." p.64, ll.20f), instances of dramatic irony (see *Glossary*), which consist in Edward's anticipation of the outcome of the play

(Flora's assigning the role of the master of the house to the matchseller). But they might also be interpreted as a sign of resignation on Edward's part: Edward, as it were, gives up control of his territory. His claim to his property a little later (p.68, l.39: "my blasted house ... my territory ...") is a last desperate attempt to maintain his position.

4. Why does Edward stop so abruptly in his speech (p.69, l.2)? At first sight, the reason for Edward's abrupt stop would seem to be the matchseller's alleged grin, which Edward refers to some moments later. But as Edward's questions, "You find that funny? Are you grinning?" (p.69, l.4), do not follow immediately (there is a pause between Edward's stopping and these reproaches), it is much more logical to say that Edward has another reason for interrupting his speech. The word that Edward started but did not finish was to have been "remember", which is made clear by Edward's taking up this thought again: "When I tell you how well I remember this room, how well I remember this den." (p.69, ll.8f). This is the beginning of the process in which Edward reveals his innermost self to the stranger, and the sentence which triggers off Edward's long monologues (p.69, ll.21–35 and p.71, ll.13–30). Evidently, in the middle of this sentence, Edward realizes that, if he continues, he will inevitably reach a point of no return, a point where he will have to explain the apparently absurd statement "I remember this room."
[Talking about the language of his plays, Pinter once said:

> I am not suggesting that no character in a play can ever say what he in fact means. Not at all. I have found that there invariably does come a moment when this happens, when he says something, perhaps, which he has never said before. And where this happens, what he says is irrevocable, and can never be taken back. ("Writing for the Theatre", p.15).

The abrupt stop in Edward's speech seems to be one of these moments Pinter refers to. The fact that Edward *imagines* that the matchseller is grinning (remember that the matchseller is wearing a balaclava, which makes it extremely difficult to determine his facial expression) shows that he anticipates the "normal" reaction to his story, and indicates that it is a reaction that fills him with the fear of making a fool of himself.]

5. In what way does Edward's speech change from now on? The stage direction *"muttering"* (p.69, l.9) indicates that Edward no longer pursues his aim of cross-examining the matchseller: he does not address himself to the stranger, but is absorbed in his own reflections. Unlike his other speeches in the play, which turned into "monologues" (or "dialogues with silence"), this passage is intended not to elicit a reaction from the old man, but to reveal Edward's innermost thoughts. (We could call this a "soliloquy" as opposed to "monologue"; cf. *Glossary*.) In this passage the pauses are not occasioned by the matchseller's failure to respond, but by Edward's rambling manner of speaking.

6. *What does Edward's soliloquy (p.69, ll.9–35) reveal about his state of mind and the way he feels?* Edward constantly refers to "yesterday" (and, as a consequence, uses the past tense throughout this passage). With the past, he associates notions like the orderliness, sharp contours and cleanliness of his surroundings, which somehow inspired him with a feeling of satisfaction and security. Edward establishes a direct connection between his once well-ordered environment and himself by taking the attribute he uses to describe things and applying it to himself: "I was polished." (p.69, l.21). Before he proceeds to the description of how he felt "yesterday", the stage direction *"nostalgic"* (p.69, l.21) indicates that what he has just said and what he is going to say belong to the past. Edward's nostalgia has already become evident in the first sentences of his soliloquy: his exclamation "Ha" (l.9) – an interjection that signals his resignation – is followed by "Yesterday now, it was clear, clearly defined, so clearly" (ll.9f) – a sentence that not only sums up the mood of his soliloquy, but also implies Edward's regret that, at the moment of speaking, there is no clear definition of the present state of affairs.

7. *The adjective "polished" is not normally used for persons. What does Edward mean when he says "I was polished"? Study the passage from l.21 to l.35.* At first sight, the reader finds himself faced with an almost never-ending sentence, divided only by commas. We get the impression that this passage does not have any logical structure, that the principle it follows can at best be called "stream of consciousness". A closer look, however, reveals a possible subdivision of this passage into five similar parts ending with "perfect" (l.24), "accounted for" (l.26), "fluent" (l. 29), "established" (l.31) and "fluent" (l.35), respectively. Each of these parts starts with an action that Edward was able to perform or used to perform. Banal as these actions and the capacity for performing them may be, they inspire Edward with a feeling of pride in his physical fitness. From this pride in his bodily strength, Edward derives a feeling of dominance and command (cf. "my command established, my life was accounted for": l.26). Of course, the connection between the different structural elements of the five parts is anything but logical. This speech can be interpreted as another sign of Edward's inferiority complex (cf. Fourth Unit), although, at this stage of his speech, Edward

is not yet willing to admit this. He finds (or rather found, as he refers to "yesterday") security and self-esteem in his being part of an unchangeable, defined environment. One critic puts it this way: "Edward has immured himself in an ultra-respectable, comfortable bourgeois existence, centred on his curio-filled house on the road, significantly enough, to a monastery. His surroundings are ordered, reduced to manageable proportions ... on his own admission he rarely goes to the village, preferring to view the outside world from the security of his own 'territory' through a telescope, which enables close scrutiny without immediate contact" (Peter C. Thornton, "Blindness and the Confrontation with Death: Three Plays by Harold Pinter", *Die Neueren Sprachen* 67 (1968), p.219).

8. Does Edward realize the futility of what he has been telling himself? At the end of l.35, as he is about to underline the fluency of his progress, he realizes that he uttered almost the same words a few moments before. Obviously, he has run out of "arguments" for his physical fitness and his command. The dropping of his arms seems like a symbol of his fading strength, an admission of defeat (he had held them up to mime a telescope, an action that used to fill him with pride in his fitness). This gesture full of resignation is immediately followed by his joining in the matchseller's (alleged?) laughter. This, rather than being another sign of friendliness towards the stranger (as p.70, ll.5f could suggest: "You're laughing with me, I'm laughing with you, we're laughing together!"), is the clearest demonstration of Edward's gnawing self-doubt. His laughter is not aimed at driving his self-doubt away, but is full of bitterness, as his sarcastic remarks show: "Laugh your bloody head off! Go on! Don't mind me. No need to be polite." (p.69, l.39). As Edward realizes in his confession that he has been living in a world of make-believe, his words "You're quite right, it is funny. I'll laugh with you!" (p.70, l.4) are a serious comment on the futility of his "yesterday" thoughts.

9. In what way does Edward's second long soliloquy (p.71, ll.13–30) add to the thoughts expressed in the first one? Edward's seclusion from the outside world, his retirement into a closed, ordered world, is symbolized by his mention of the canopy, which he used to erect in a shadowy corner (under a tree or behind a bush) to shelter himself from any outside influence ("Nothing entered, nothing left my nook." p.72, ll.22f). This refuge provided him with a feeling of security and protection, and allowed him to live in complete harmony with nature (as his physical contact with the blades of grass and the petals testifies). In this "still life", Edward's role is entirely passive ("Things happened upon me": p.71, ll.27f). [It would be quite acceptable to liken Edward's position in his nook to the life of a baby in the womb in the pre-natal phase; cf. Wilfried Uhlmann, "Neurotische Konflikte und triebgesteuertes Sozialverhalten in den Stücken Harold Pinters", *Literatur in Wissenschaft und Unterricht* 5 (1972), p.304.] Also with regard to the tone of voice Edward adopts, the second part of this soliloquy forms a parallel to his first soliloquy. Edward's fading voice (*"low murmur"*; ll.21f) shows that he is merely talking to himself and evoking happy memories of the past.

10. What, according to Edward, disturbed the peace and quiet of his own world? Immediately after his reminiscences about the complacency of the past, Edward explicitly mentions the reason for the disturbance of his peace: "But then, the time came. I saw the wind, swirling, and the dust at my back gate, lifting, and the long grass, scything together" (p.71, ll.32f). These movements (the dramatic effect of which is heightened by the unusual position of the participles) clearly meant a destruction of Edward's idyllic ordered world. The dust lifted by the swirling wind is a menace to this refuge as it destroys his "polished"world. Dust, then, is the direct counterpart to "polished" – the word that Edward used to describe his "yesterday" world.

11. How does the matchseller fit into this picture? The soliloquy shows that Edward felt secure in his "polished" world as long as there was no intrusion from outside. The fact that the place where the threatening dust rose is the back gate (cf. p.71, ll. 32f) is significant, being the place where the matchseller stopped for so long. Edward's remark, "Seeing you stand, at the back gate, such close proximity, was not at all the same thing." (p.70, ll.18f), establishes the connection between the old man and the dust: the matchseller's presence, too, is an intrusion into Edward's world. In addition, he is an intruder whose identity is unknown and so resists Edward's need of clear definitions (cf. p.69, ll.9f). The two threats to Edward's complacent world also share another element: the notion of dirt normally associated with dust finds its equivalent in the grubby outward appearance of the matchseller.
It might be argued as to whether we are entitled to refer to *two* threats: the dust at the back gate may simply be linked with the matchseller at the back gate by simple association in Edward's stream-of-consciousness talk. There can be no doubt, however, as to the meaning of the dust/dirt and the matchseller: they are a kind of physical manifestation of Edward's deeply ingrained fear of anything that might disturb his complacent world. As for the matchseller alone, he could be termed a catalyst who brings Edward's anxieties to the surface.

12. Discuss the meaning of the "slight ache" in Edward's eyes, which gives the play its title. Edward attributes the slight ache in his eyes to a germ he has been infected with: "A germ. In my eyes. It was this morning." (p.71, ll.10f). This weakness due to an infection "this morning" is in sharp contrast with the physical fitness he claims to have had "yesterday". So, its relation to the threat Edward feels is immediately established by the time adverbial "this morning". Given the fact that germs are transported by the wind (considered as an enemy by Edward), it can be said that the slight ache is the physical consequence of the threat of intrusion that Edward feels. [Uhlmann, *op.cit.*, p.303, talks of a "conversion" in the psychiatric sense of the word, i.e. the conversion of a psychological conflict into a physical symptom (in this case an ache in the eyes), as is typical of persons suffering from hysteria.] Despite the apparent importance given by the title of the play to this slight ache, it should not be forgotten that Edward complains of other symptoms as well: "fever" and "a cold" (p.71, ll.9f). All this could be symptomatic of an allergic illness. Thus it might be said that Edward's illness is the physical expression of a psychic allergy to all influences from the outside world, the matchseller being one of them.
The "slight ache" in Edward's eyes is also related to the theme of blindness. At the beginning of the play, Edward had derived a sense of power and satisfaction from "blinding" (p.53, l.40) the wasp. He again refers to this incident in his first soliloquy, giving it as an example of the things he could do when he was still in full possession of his faculties: "I could pour hot water down the spoon hole, yes, easily, ..." (p.69, ll.24f). Now, however, it seems that he is being blinded, deprived of his faculties and caught like the wasp. (Cf. Ann P. Messenger, "Blindness and the Problem of Identity in Pinter's Plays." *Die Neueren Sprachen* 71 (1972), 481–490.)

13. What makes Edward refer to the matchseller as his "oldest acquaintance", his "nearest and dearest", his "kith and kin" (p.70, ll.11f)? As has already been hinted at above, Edward tends to identify himself with the matchseller. The stranger becomes a projection of the menace within Edward himself, a catalyst who brings his anxiety to the surface. Edward's self-imposed exile and seclusion are due to his fear of the outside world. The matchseller then becomes an embodiment of these fears, which have been smoldering just below the surface for a long time ("oldest acquaintance"), and are part and parcel of his life ("nearest and dearest", "kith and kin".)
As soon as the matchseller appears at the back gate, Edward realizes that it is no longer any use trying to keep reality (his own fears) at bay. Up to that moment, he has succeeded in avoiding the direct confrontation with reality;

the world outside was miles away and only existed as a remote object he watched through a telescope. Edward's desire to keep the outside world – and the matchseller – at a distance is also evident in his remarks "... correspondence would have been as satisfactory ... We could have exchanged postcards ..." (p.70, ll.12f), as letters and postcards, too, establish contact with another part of the world, but remove the necessity for face-to-face contact. It is the matchseller's presence at the back gate, i.e. the frontier between Edward's and the outside world, that makes Edward realize that the confrontation with reality cannot now be avoided – a realization which provokes anxiety and fear within him: "Seeing you stand, at the back gate, *such close proximity*, was not at all the same thing." (p.70, ll.18f; italics added). This realization drives Edward to the point of neurosis. It is not only the mystery of the matchseller's identity that makes him feel afraid, but also his imagining that the old man changes every time he sees him: "In fact every time I have seen you you have looked quite different to the time before." (p.70, ll.28f), which adds to the menace and mystery that the stranger represents for Edward.
On the other hand, Edward seems to have given up the idea of finding out about the matchseller's identity (but cf. Edward's question "Who are you?"; p.72, ll.13, which seems to contradict this). He no longer insists that the stranger should take off his balaclava, which hides part of his face, claiming that he has seen him without it anyway (cf. p.70, ll.22–26). From Edward's enumeration of the times and circumstances in which he claims to have seen the matchseller (p.70, ll.33–38), it becomes evident that the stranger must *always* have been there and that he is indeed Edward's *alter ego.* Another hint that Edward and the matchseller are really one and the same is provided when Edward tells the stranger to blow his nose, then blows his own nose a little while later (cf. p.71, ll.7, 9f).

14. How can we interpret the fact that, during his soliloquy, Edward has a breakdown? Edward's soliloquy contains the surrender of his command over his territory. The psychological breakdown finds its physical correlate in his breakdown in the last scene. He falls to the floor (p.71, l.12); a few moments later, his voice becomes weaker (p.72, l.4), and his last utterance in the play is to be rendered as a *"great final effort – a whisper"* (p.71, l.13). Given the fact that Edward's self-esteem and command were founded on his physical fitness, we can say that his collapse comes at the moment when he realizes that he is no longer able to explain his "territory" because he is no longer in command of it; certainly, the use of the conditional in "I would like to join you ... explain ... show you ... the garden ... explain ... The plants ..." (p.72, ll.4f) is not meant to express a wish, but obviously has to be completed by the if-clause "if I only could"!

15. In what way does the matchseller change in the last scene? In Edward's eyes, the matchseller has become younger (p.72, l.1). His rejuvenation (and thus his readiness for the assumption of command) is diametrically opposed to Edward's ailing and weak appearance and so prepares the way for the role-reversal at the end of the play. The "stripling" that Edward sees in the old man reminds him of his own youth and his career as a sprinter when he was able to defeat men twice his strength (cf. p.72, ll.6–8). Now, he is a loser who is not even able to "defeat" an old man. He seems to have inherited the very characteristics that he used to describe the matchseller: once, he boasted of his supremacy over the matchseller by telling Flora, "He can't see straight." (p.65, l.4) and insisting on the old man's weakness ("He's very nearly dead on his feet." p.65, l.6); now he himself suffers from a slight ache in his eyes and experiences a breakdown. Edward has changed places with the matchseller.

16. Edward's breakdown can be called the climax of the play. Why then, does it not constitute the very end of the play? In several respects, Flora's return to the stage underlines Edward's defeat. Whereas Edward is still puzzled by the question of the matchseller's identity ("Who are you?": p.72, l.13), Flora has already solved this problem by baptizing the old man "Barnabas", which is a sign of the beginning of her supremacy over her husband. The juxtaposition of Edward's question and Flora's calling the matchseller from off stage by a name produces a comic effect: Flora's call seems like an answer to Edward's question, but, as it does not solve Edward's problem, seems to ridicule his quest for a solution.
While Edward found himself unable to explain his "territory" to the matchseller, Flora is eager to show him her garden (cf. p.72, ll.18f; note the use of the possessive "my"; Flora's invitation to the matchseller may well have an obscene meaning). The garden has become her "territory".
Flora has already substituted the matchseller for Edward: her husband is no longer the master of the house. Now, it is the matchseller's garden ("... your garden": p.72, l.18). She does the same things for the old man that she once offered to do for Edward. In fact, she uses almost the same words as in a previous scene with Edward (compare p.72, ll.21f and p.64, ll.13f). The fact that she puts the matchseller's tray in Edward's hands is a final gesture which completes the reversal of roles between Edward and the old man. Flora clearly demonstrates to her husband that she has no further use for

him. For her, Edward has become as irrelevant as a matchseller with wet and mouldy matches.

17. Interpret Flora's statement "The summer is coming." (p.72, l.21) and the other references to time on this page. Of course, the summer has already arrived and has even reached its height. In Flora's imagination, however, the time of happiness with the matchseller in Edward's stead is only just beginning. So, the summer symbolizes a sort of new life, a rebirth for Flora. Thanks to the "dream man" at her side, the time of year in which the flowers are in full bloom will also allow Flora (= the flower) to bloom with satisfaction and happiness. When applied to Edward's situation the season symbolism might be interpreted in the following manner: Edward's self-esteem and complacency (his "summer", so to speak) end on this longest day of the year; for him, the height of summer will be followed "by inevitable decline into autumn and winter" (cf. Thornton, *op.cit.*, p.220). A similar interpretation can be based on the references to the time of the day. Whereas Edward's day has come to an end (cf. his references to the moonlight), for Flora it is the height of the day ("You can *lunch* in the garden ..."; p.72, ll.21f; italics added).

Blackboard (see p. 153)

Homework

As the last unit might have proved extremely difficult (especially the disentanglement of the images at the end), homework consisting of the reproduction of the results obtained in the Sixth Unit is not recommended. Instead the pupils could be asked

1. to judge (and, if need be, expand or even correct) the interpretations of passages dealt with in Units 1–5 in the light of their understanding of the last unit. Questions such as the following might also be part of a test:
   a) At the beginning of the play, Edward does not recognize the flowers in his garden (cf. p.50, l.9–p.51, l.7). Comment.
   (→ foreboding of the outcome of the last scene where Edward's inability to explain his garden is the sign of his loss of command over his "territory").
   b) Why does Edward refer to the weather (sunny, with a light breeze) as treacherous (p.51, l.16)? (→ symbolic meaning of the wind: change, movement, which Edward is afraid of).

c) What new aspects does the Sixth Unit add to the wasp episode? (wasp = intrusion of a "stranger" into Edward's world → Edward's first complaint of a slight ache in his eyes = his allergy to any influence from the outside world; see the simultaneity of the wasps's arrival and the first occurrence of Edward's slight ache (pp.51f); the killing of the wasp (p.54, l.3) is one of the actions that fill Edward with pride in his physical fitness (cf. p.69, ll.24f) and his command; hence his glee after the torture and killing of this intruder into his world).

d) Explain Edward's "toneless" reaction to Flora's search for him in the attic and in the toolshed (p.55, l.38 and p.56, l.6, respectively). (→ Edward's fear of being considered by Flora as a useless and old-fashioned object that is removed to the attic and falls into oblivion, or a tool handled by Flora according to her will. Obviously, the depressed state of mind Edward is in while watching the matchseller from the scullery provides him with a vague anticipation of the fact that he is going to have to surrender his command and will be cast off by Flora at the end of the play).

2. to try and apply some passages from literary critics to the whole of the play. The pupils could be given the following homework: "Discuss one of the following statements in the light of our interpretation of *A Slight Ache.*"

[The attention of the audience of a Pinter play] is held by small, disconnected incidents while the play-long interests are being manifested at a different level of consciousness ... The audience ... may discern a progressive disclosure of antagonisms, desires or appetites which were hidden at the beginning.
J. R. Brown, "Mr. Pinter's Shakespeare", *The Critical Quarterly* 5, No. 3 (Autumn 1963), p.251.

In absurd drama, language is obscure or irrelevant; silence is frequent. When the silent character is introduced, the speaking characters instinctively feel threatened by the mysteriously silent one. They attempt to minimize the threat, but the vehemence of their endeavours serves only to intensify the menace ... the silent characters are passive vehicles for the projections of the talking ones.
K. F. Stein, "Metaphysical Silence in Absurd Drama", *Modern Drama* 13 (1971), p.425.

[Pinter's] general strategy is progressive discovery ... The conclusion is often marked by ... a shift of power that had been working surreptitiously throughout the action ...
J. R. Brown, *Theatre Language. A Study of Arden, Osborne, Pinter and Wesker*, London 1972, p.95.

Blackboard

"Yesterday"/Pretence

Edward's world and his command over it:

- the well-ordered and unchangeable nature of his surroundings (Edward's being in harmony with nature)
- "polished"
- his avoidance of direct contact with the world outside (symbols: telescope; postcards, correspondence)
- his physical fitness

Edward's feeling of shelter and security, self-esteem and complacency in his self-imposed exile

"Today"/Reality

The real world invades his territory:

movement, change: the swirling wind

lifting the dust *at the back gate*

dirt *at the back gate*

the dirty matchseller *at the back gate*
= intrusion into Edward's world

(transporting) the germ

a slight ache/fever: allergy to all influences from outside

a threat that acts as a catalyst for Edward's deeply ingrained fear of the outside world

conversion of a psychological conflict into a physical defect

Clash of two worlds

Edward's breakdown (awareness of the inevitability of a confrontation with the outside world)

Glossary of Literary Terms

Action: The series of events initiated by the characters in a play. It usually consists of *rising action, climax* and *falling action.*
Actor: The person playing a character on stage. His performance is guided by the director and represents an interpretation of the character.
Antagonist: see *Protagonist.*
Character: A person in a play or other literary work.
Climax: Moment at which the action comes to its point of greatest intensity. It marks the turning point of the action.
Dénouement: The resolution of the conflicts in a play.
Dialogue: The conversation between two or more characters.
Director: The person responsible for a performance of a play on stage.
Dramatic irony: The words or actions of a character in a play may carry a meaning unperceived by himself but understood by the audience. The irony lies in the contrast between the meaning intended by the speaker and the added significance seen by others, e.g. when Edward in *A Slight Ache* says about the matchseller, "I should be the same perhaps, in his place", he anticipates the outcome of the play.
Euphemism: The use of an indirect or vague expression for a word which is thought to be offensive or vulgar.
Exposition: That part of the play where background information on the characters and the situation is provided (usually given at the beginning of the play).
Falling action: That part of the play which leads to the resolution of the action. It follows the *climax* and leads to the *dénouement.*
Flat/round character: Flat characters have only one "side". Their behaviour is predictable and they present one single characteristic trait. Round characters are "rounded out", i.e. they have many "sides" and usually show a certain development in their character.
Irony: A figure of speech where the actual meaning of what is said is hidden behind the obvious statement. It is often used with a humorous or satirical intention.
Metaphor: A figure of speech connecting two different, and basically incompatible, things which have a common ground of comparison, e.g. the quality of continuity and rapid flow in the expression "the river of life".
Monologue: A long speech by one character, heard but not interrupted by the other characters. (Cf. *Soliloquy).*
One-act play: A short play concentrating on a single dramatic situation and aiming at a single dramatic effect. When compared to a full-length play, the

structural elements of time, space, character and action appear in a reduced form.

Play within the play: A theatrical performance as part of the play's action, showing the characters of the play as spectators. It is usually employed to confront the audience with their own situation as spectators, e.g. the TV play in James Saunders' *A Slight Accident.*

Plot: The basic structure of the play's action, quite often a causal sequence of events.

Props: Short for "stage properties": articles (e.g. pieces of furniture) used on stage.

Protagonist: The main character of the play; the character around whom the action of the play is centred. His opponent is the antagonist.

Rising action: That part of the play which brings about the complication, i.e. the part in which the opposing forces meet. It follows the *exposition* and leads to the *climax* of the play.

Round character: see *Flat character.*

Scene: Subdivision of a play usually marked by a change of place or the entry or exit of a character. Traditionally: subdivision of an act.

Scenery: The overall picture of the stage comprising *props* and *stage design.*

Setting: The place and time of the action.

Soliloquy: A long speech by one character, which is not meant to be overheard by the other characters and in which he reveals his thoughts to the audience. (Cf. *Monologue*).

Stage design: The decoration of the stage conveying the place, the time and the atmosphere of the play.

Stage direction: That part of the dramatic text which gives information as to how the place and atmosphere of a play are to be imagined or how a speech is to be rendered.

Theatre of the absurd: Dramatic style in which the traditional conceptions of character, plot, time sequence and dialogue are deliberately disregarded. The theatre of the absurd describes human life as purposeless.

Bibliography

1. Reference Books

Abrams, M. H. *A Glossary of Literary Terms.* (3rd ed.) New York 1971.

Bodenschatz, Herbert. *Englisches Lernwörterbuch zur Textanalyse.* Frankfurt/M. 1979.

Fowler, Rodger, ed. *A Dictionary of Modern Critical Terms.* London 1973.

Werlich, Egon. *Wörterbuch der Textinterpretation. The Field System Dictionary for Text Analysis.* (8th print.) Dortmund 1978.

2. General

Hayman, Ronald. *British Theatre since 1955. A Reassessment.* Oxford 1979.

Hayman, Ronald. *How to Read a Play.* London 1977.

"Hörspiel und Kurzdrama." *Der fremdsprachliche Unterricht* 49 (1979).

Ingarden, Roman. "Von den Funktionen der Sprache im Theaterschauspiel", in: *Das literarische Kunstwerk.* Tübingen 1965.

Pfister, Manfred. *Das Drama, Theorie und Analyse.* München 1977.

Schik, Berthold. "Das Drama im Englischunterricht der reformierten Oberstufe: Vorschläge zu einem Interpretationsverfahren." *Literatur in Wissenschaft und Unterricht.* Beiheft zu Band 11 (1978), 38–53.

Schik, Berthold. "Das Kurzdrama im Fremdsprachenunterricht." *Der fremdsprachliche Unterricht* 49 (1979), 16–27.

Scholes, Robert and Carl H. Klaus. *Elements of Drama.* New York 1971.

Taylor, John Russell. *Anger and After. A Guide to the New British Drama.* London 1962.

Taylor, John Russell. *The Second Wave. British Drama for the Seventies.* London 1971.

3. Tom Stoppard

Bigsby, C. W. E. *Tom Stoppard.* Harlow 1976.

Hayman, Ronald. *Tom Stoppard.* London 1977.

Stoppard, Tom. "Ambushes for the Audience: Towards a High Comedy of Ideas – An Interview." *Theatre Quarterly*, May–July 1974, 3–17.

4. James Saunders

Hayman, Ronald. "Commentary". In: *Neighbours and Other Plays by James Saunders.* London 1968, pp.163–71.

Spiel, Hilde. "Im Strom des Absurden. James Saunders: Ein Porträt." *Die Zeit* 37 (10. 9. 1965), 18–20.

5. Harold Pinter

Amend, Victor E. "Harold Pinter – Some Credits and Debits." *Modern Drama* 10 (1967/68), 165–174.

Brown, J. R. "Mr. Pinter's Shakespeare." *The Critical Quarterly* 5, No. 3 (Autumn 1963), 251–265.

Brown, J. R. *Theatre Language. A Study of Arden, Osborne, Pinter and Wesker.* London 1972.

Esslin, Martin. *Pinter: A Study of his Plays.* London 1970.

Goetsch, Paul. "Pinter. A Slight Ache." In: Prießnitz, H. P., ed. *Das englische Hörspiel.* Düsseldorf 1977, pp.101–113, 370f.

Hinchliffe, Arnold P. *Harold Pinter.* New York 1967.

Imhof, Rüdiger. *Harold Pinters Dramentechnik. Gestalterische Mittel im Kontext des Gesamtwerks.* Bonn 1976.

Messenger, Ann P. "Blindness and the Problem of Identity in Pinter's Plays." *Die Neueren Sprachen* 71 (1972), 481–490.

Müller-Zannoth, I. *Der Dialog in Harold Pinters Dramen. Aspekte seiner kommunikativen Funktion.* Bern 1977.

Nagel, Regine. "Kurzdramen Pinters im Leistungskurs der Sekundarstufe II." *Der Fremdsprachliche Unterricht* 49 (1979), 49–59.

Pinter, Harold. "Writing for the Theatre." In: Pinter, Harold. *Plays. One.* London 1976, pp.9–16.

Prießnitz, H. P. *Das englische "radio play" seit 1945. Typen, Themen und Formen.* Berlin 1978.

Stein, Karen F. "Metaphysical Silence in Absurd Drama." *Modern Drama* 13 (1971), 423–431.

Thornton, Peter C. "Blindness and the Confrontation with Death: Three Plays by Harold Pinter." *Die Neueren Sprachen* 67 (1968), 213–223.

Uhlmann, Wilfried. "Neurotische Konflikte und triebgesteuertes Sozialverhalten in den Stücken Harold Pinters." *Literatur in Wissenschaft und Unterricht* 5 (1972), 299–312.